# 150 HOUSES

**YOU NEED
TO VISIT BEFORE
YOU DIE**

Lannoo

#architecturehunting #architecturelover #architectureporn: check those hashtags on Instagram and you'll realise, architecture tourism is on the rise. Unsurprisingly perhaps: architecture is photogenic. But if you also get a chance to see what's hiding behind the façade, the experience is truly inspirational. Is there anything more fun than peeking into original interiors? Especially if those homes were designed by a world-renowned architect?

Journalist Thijs Demeulemeester and art and architecture historian Jacinthe Gigou are both crazy about 20th-century architecture. Together they drew up a shortlist of 150 stunning 20th-century homes that are open to visitors. Most are house museums with fixed opening hours. Others can be rented as Airbnb. And some are hidden treasures, which you can visit by appointment only.

If you're taking a road trip through southern France, which architectural marvels are worth the detour? Which houses should you see during your city getaway in São Paolo? Which pearls of residential architecture can you visit in Paris? What is the equivalent of Le Corbusier's Villa Savoye in Norway? And if you are planning an architecture trip to, say, Palm Springs, which architectural masterpieces should you most definitely book in advance? Let *150 houses you need to visit before you die* be your guide.

Unlike (art) museums, 'house museums' are often lesser-known gems. They won't be featured in every tourist guide. Finding them or gaining access takes quite a bit of research. This book solves that problem. The authors scoured the world for 150 must-see modern private homes from the 20th century. So call *150 houses you need to visit before you die* an architectural bucket list. Or a TO DO list for lovers of 20th-century residential architecture. Anyone who has visited all 150 houses, raise your hand. There's a surprise waiting for you.

## OVERVIEW

# AFRICA

### MOROCCO
| | | |
|---|---|---|
| 001 | **VILLA MAJORELLE** | p.10 |
| 002 | **VILLA RONDE** | p.14 |
| 003 | **VILLA ZEVACO** | p.16 |

# THE AMERICAS

### BRAZIL
| | | |
|---|---|---|
| 004 | **CASA DAS CANOAS** | p.18 |
| 005 | **CASA ABERTA** | p.19 |
| 006 | **CASA VILANOVA ARTIGAS** | p.22 |
| 007 | **CASA OSCAR AMERICANO** | p.23 |
| 008 | **CASA DE VIDRO / THE GLASS HOUSE** | p.26 |
| 009 | **CASA WALTHER MOREIRA SALLES** | p.30 |
| 010 | **CASA MODERNISTA** | p.32 |

### CANADA
| | | |
|---|---|---|
| 011 | **HABITAT 67** | p.34 |

### MEXICO
| | | |
|---|---|---|
| 012 | **CASA BARRAGÁN** | p.38 |
| 013 | **CASA AZUL / THE BLUE HOUSE** | p.39 |
| 014 | **CASA ESTUDIO DIEGO RIVERA Y FRIDA KAHLO** | p.40 |
| 015 | **CASA O'GORMAN** | p.42 |
| 016 | **CASA ORGÁNICA** | p.46 |

### USA
| | | |
|---|---|---|
| 017 | **ALAN I W FRANK HOUSE** | p.50 |
| 018 | **ALDEN B. DOW HOME AND STUDIO** | p.51 |
| 019 | **JUDD FOUNDATION** | p.52 |
| 020 | **EAMES HOUSE** | p.53 |
| 021 | **ELROD HOUSE** | p.54 |
| 022 | **FALLINGWATER HOUSE** | p.55 |
| 023 | **FARNSWORTH HOUSE** | p.58 |
| 024 | **FRANK LLOYD WRIGHT HOUSE / THE KRAUS HOUSE** | p.59 |
| 025 | **FRANK SINATRA HOUSE** | p.60 |
| 026 | **FREDERICK C. ROBIE HOUSE** | p.61 |
| 027 | **FREY HOUSE II** | p.62 |
| 028 | **GAMBLE HOUSE** | p.62 |
| 029 | **GARCIA HOUSE** | p.64 |
| 030 | **GHOST RANCH** | p.64 |
| 031 | **GRACE MILLER HOUSE** | p.66 |
| 032 | **THE GLASS HOUSE** | p.66 |
| 033 | **GROPIUS HOUSE** | p.70 |
| 034 | **HOLLYHOCK HOUSE** | p.72 |
| 035 | **JAMES ROSE CENTER** | p.74 |
| 036 | **KENTUCK KNOB** | p.75 |
| 037 | **KORMAN HOUSE** | p.78 |
| 038 | **LILJESTRAND HOUSE** | p.80 |
| 039 | **MANITOGA** | p.81 |
| 040 | **BERNARD SCHWARTZ HOUSE / STILL BEND** | p.82 |
| 041 | **MILLER HOUSE** | p.84 |
| 042 | **THE MODULIGHTOR BUILDING** | p.86 |
| 043 | **HARVEY HOUSE** | p.87 |
| 044 | **NEUTRA VDL HOUSE** | p.88 |

# OVERVIEW

| | | |
|---|---|---|
| 045 | PALMER HOUSE | p.89 |
| 046 | THE SHEATS - GOLDSTEIN HOUSE | p.90 |
| 047 | PRAIRIE HOUSE | p.94 |
| 048 | SCHINDLER HOUSE | p.95 |
| 049 | SAARINEN HOUSE | p.96 |
| 050 | WICHITA / DYMAXION HOUSE | p.97 |
| 051 | TYLER RESIDENCE | p.98 |
| 052 | STAHL HOUSE / CASE STUDY HOUSE #22 | p.99 |
| 053 | TALIESIN EAST & WEST | p.100 |
| 054 | UMBRELLA HOUSE | p.104 |

### VENEZUELA
| | | |
|---|---|---|
| 055 | VILLA PLANCHART | p.106 |

## ASIA

### INDIA
| | | |
|---|---|---|
| 056 | JEANNERET HOUSE | p.108 |

### ISRAEL
| | | |
|---|---|---|
| 057 | WEIZMANN HOUSE | p.109 |

### SRI LANKA
| | | |
|---|---|---|
| 058 | BAWA HOUSE | p.110 |
| 059 | LUNUGANGA | p.111 |

## EUROPE

### AUSTRIA
| | | |
|---|---|---|
| 060 | DOMENIG STEINHAUS | p.112 |
| 061 | VILLA BEER | p.116 |

### BELGIUM
| | | |
|---|---|---|
| 062 | HÔTEL MAX HALLET | p.117 |
| 063 | HORTA MUSEUM | p.118 |
| 064 | HÔTEL SOLVAY | p.120 |
| 065 | HÔTEL OTLET | p.121 |
| 066 | VILLA EMPAIN | p.122 |
| 067 | MAISON BERTEAUX | p.126 |
| 068 | DE BEIR HOUSE / 'BLACK HOUSE' | p.128 |
| 069 | RENAAT BRAEM HOUSE | p.130 |

### CZECH REPUBLIC
| | | |
|---|---|---|
| 070 | BRUMMEL HOUSE | p.132 |
| 071 | VILLA WINTERNITZ | p.133 |
| 072 | THE HIRSCH APARTMENT | p.134 |
| 073 | VILLA MÜLLER | p.134 |

### DENMARK
| | | |
|---|---|---|
| 074 | FINN JUHL'S HUS | p.136 |

### FINLAND
| | | |
|---|---|---|
| 075 | AALTO HOUSE | p.137 |
| 076 | FUTURO HOUSE | p.138 |
| 077 | HVITTRÄSK | p.140 |
| 078 | VILLA MAIREA | p.141 |
| 079 | MUURATSALO EXPERIMENTAL HOUSE | p.142 |

# OVERVIEW

## FRANCE

| | | |
|---|---|---|
| 080 | LE CABANON | p.143 |
| 081 | HÔTEL MARTEL | p.144 |
| 082 | LOUIS CARRÉ HOUSE | p.146 |
| 083 | MAISONS LA ROCHE-JEANNERET | p.150 |
| 084 | MAISON UNAL | p.152 |
| 085 | PALACIO DE ABRAXAS | p.156 |
| 086 | POSTMAN CHEVAL'S IDEAL PALACE | p.158 |
| 087 | RÉSIDENCE LE POINT DU JOUR | p.159 |
| 088 | PRIVATE RESIDENCE OF JEAN PROUVÉ | p.160 |
| 089 | THE 'RADIANT CITY' HOUSING UNIT | p.161 |
| 090 | STUDIO-APARTMENT OF LE CORBUSIER | p.162 |
| 091 | STUDIO-HOME OF THEO VAN DOESBURG | p.166 |
| 092 | VILLA CAVROIS | p.168 |
| 093 | VILLA E-1027 | p.170 |
| 094 | VILLA FALBALA | p.171 |
| 095 | VILLA MAJORELLE | p.172 |
| 096 | VILLA ON THE ROCKS | p.174 |
| 097 | VILLA NOAILLES | p.175 |
| 098 | VILLA SAVOYE | p.176 |

## GERMANY

| | | |
|---|---|---|
| 099 | HAUS AM HORN | p.178 |
| 100 | HAUS HOHE PAPPELN | p.180 |
| 101 | HOHENHOF | p.181 |
| 102 | HAUS LANGE AND HAUS ESTERS | p.182 |
| 103 | HAUS UNGERS | p.183 |
| 104 | VILLA STUCK | p.184 |
| 105 | MASTERS' HOUSES | p.186 |
| 106 | SCHMINKE HOUSE | p.188 |
| 107 | WEISSENHOFSIEDLUNG | p.192 |
| 108 | TAUT'S HAUS | p.193 |

## ITALY

| | | |
|---|---|---|
| 109 | CASA CRESPI | p.194 |
| 110 | CASA REMO BRINDISI | p.195 |
| 111 | CASA SALDARINI | p.196 |
| 112 | VILLA BORSANI | p.198 |
| 113 | VILLA NECCHI-CAMPIGLIO | p.199 |
| 114 | VILLA LEONI | p.200 |
| 115 | VILLA OTTOLENGHI | p.202 |

## THE NETHERLANDS

| | | |
|---|---|---|
| 116 | DIAGOON HOUSING | p.204 |
| 117 | JAN DE JONG HOUSE | p.206 |
| 118 | WALL HOUSE #2 | p.207 |
| 119 | SONNEVELD HOUSE | p.210 |
| 120 | VAN SCHIJNDEL HOUSE | p.212 |
| 121 | KIEFHOEK RESIDENCE | p.214 |
| 122 | SCHRÖDER HOUSE | p.215 |
| 123 | JACHTHUIS SINT HUBERTUS | p.216 |

## NORWAY

| | | |
|---|---|---|
| 124 | VILLA STENERSEN | p.217 |

## POLAND

| | | |
|---|---|---|
| 125 | KERET HOUSE | p.218 |
| 126 | OSKAR HANSEN HOUSE | p.220 |

# OVERVIEW

| | PORTUGAL | |
|---|---|---|
| 127 | **CASA DAS MARINHAS** | p.222 |
| 128 | **VILLA SERRALVES** | p.223 |

| | RUSSIA | |
|---|---|---|
| 129 | **GORKY HOUSE** | p.224 |
| 130 | **MELNIKOV HOUSE** | p.225 |

| | SLOVENIA | |
|---|---|---|
| 131 | **PLECNIK HOUSE** | p.226 |

| | SPAIN | |
|---|---|---|
| 132 | **CAN LIS** | p.227 |
| 133 | **CASA BATTLÓ** | p.228 |
| 134 | **CASA MILÀ** | p.228 |
| 135 | **CASA VICENS** | p.230 |
| 136 | **LA FÀBRICA** | p.231 |
| 137 | **LA RICARDA / THE GOMIS HOUSE** | p.234 |
| 138 | **SOLO HOUSE** | p.235 |
| 139 | **VOLCANO HOUSE** | p.236 |

| | SWITZERLAND | |
|---|---|---|
| 140 | **HAUS DULDECK** | p.237 |
| 141 | **MAISON BLANCHE** | p.238 |
| 142 | **VILLA "LE LAC"** | p.239 |

| | UNITED KINGDOM | |
|---|---|---|
| 143 | **BARBICAN ESTATE** | p.240 |
| 144 | **BLACKWELL** | p.241 |
| 145 | **CHARLESTON HOUSE** | p.242 |
| 146 | **ELTHAM PALACE** | p.243 |
| 147 | **THE HILL HOUSE** | p.244 |

# OCEANIA

| | AUSTRALIA | |
|---|---|---|
| 148 | **BOYD II RESIDENCE** | p.246 |
| 149 | **BUTTERFLY HOUSE** | p.247 |
| 150 | **ROSE SEIDLER HOUSE** | p.250 |

Africa — Morocco

# 01 VILLA OASIS (1923)

By Robert Poisson and Paul Sinoir
Rue Yves St Laurent, Marrakech 40090, Morocco (15)

TO VISIT BEFORE YOU DIE BECAUSE

Witness the house where Yves Saint Laurent would design his haute couture collections.

A veritable Eden in the heart of Marrakech, the Villa Oasis and its lush 9000 m² garden form an oasis of intense blue, the favourite colour of the painter Jacques Majorelle (1886 - 1962), who settled here in 1929. The son of the Art Nouveau cabinetmaker Louis Majorelle, Jacques suffered from a lung disease that forced him to settle in hot countries. He chose to live in Marrakech, where he bought a palm grove in 1922, and had a Moorish Art Deco villa built by the architects Robert Poisson and Paul Sinoir. It was here that he set up home, as well as a huge studio in which to paint his immense orientalist decorations. It was only in 1937 that he painted it with the intense shade of indigo blue to which he gave his name: Majorelle Blue. Passionate about botany, he created a garden of tropical species, like a living painting, which he made open to the public in 1947. When he died, the villa and its garden were left abandoned. Yves Saint Laurent and Pierre Bergé fell under the spell of this lost paradise, which the couple went on to buy in 1980.

Africa — Morocco

## 02 VILLA RONDE (1963–1965)

By Wolfgang Ewerth
Rue D'Anfa Superieur, Casablanca, Morocco (90)

**TO VISIT BEFORE YOU DIE BECAUSE**

This sci-fi villa offers a fantasised, optimistic, and joyful vision of sixties architecture.

Situated upon the hill of Anfa in Casablanca, the Villa Ronde is the archetypal expression of 1960s modernity. Like a UFO from outer space, Doctor B's Villa – or the 'Camembert' Villa as the Casablanca locals tend to call it – is a perfect glass-fronted 360° circle, offering multiple views of the ocean and the tropical garden. Designed by the German architect Wolfgang Ewerth (1905 - around 1976), it combines tradition and modernity, in the materials used as much as for the shape of the design. A traditional Moroccan living room is situated on the ground floor, featuring zellige tilework, stucco, and carved-wood decorations. Upstairs, there is an almost futuristic bias, with acidulous colours: pink and yellow bathrooms, and a blue kitchen. Beautiful wood-relief panelling decorates the walls, geometric cut-outs dress the ceilings, and large bay-windows open out onto the beauty of the Atlantic. A circular pool populated by water lilies is positioned in front of the entrance of the house and echoes it. The circle appears once more, at the back, in the form of the pool produced in reinforced concrete.

# 03 VILLA ZEVACO (1947)

By Jean-François Zevaco,
restored by Andy Martin Studio, Corner Boulevard D'Anfa / Casablanca, Morocco

TO VISIT BEFORE YOU DIE BECAUSE

This villa is a cultural reference point for the people of Casablanca.

This was one of the first villas to appear in Casablanca after the war, and it was a building that helped introduce the principle of modernity into Moroccan architecture. Sponsored by Sami Suissa, the businessman who originally gave his name to the house, it is better known today under the name of Villa Zevaco, a name inherited from the sign for restoration that was installed there. Located at a crossroads at the entrance to the chic neighbourhood of Anfa, it presents a very plastic sculptural façade, with its subtly flared curved line - to which it owes the nickname of the 'Butterfly Villa'. The Villa Zevaco fully expresses the optimism of the fast approaching 1950s, with its dynamic lines and modern amenities. It blends several references: Corbusian brutalism, Californian avant-garde, and Brazilian lyricism. It is one of a series of highly original buildings by Jean-François Zevaco (1916–2003), a French architect born in Casablanca, who was to continue building in the 'white city' until the 1980s. After the death of Zevaco in 2003, the house has been transformed into a coffee bar.

The Americas — Brazil

## 04 CASA DAS CANOAS (1951)

By Oscar Niemeyer
Estrada das Canoas, No. 2310, São Conrado,
Rio de Janeiro, Brazil

TO VISIT BEFORE YOU DIE BECAUSE

This refined and forward-thinking masterpiece from Niemeyer was fit to be his home.

The master of lyrical Brazilian architecture, Oscar Niemeyer (1907–2012), built his personal home in a lush forest near the ocean in Rio. With its light and very open constructive dynamic, it seems to have been discreetly placed in the heart of nature. The designer of Brasilia and a great humanist, Niemeyer is part of the second generation of Modernist architects. He embodies a form of architecture that is very poetic and highly inventive in terms of its forms, which he prefers to keep free and sensual. He stands out strongly from pioneers of the movement such as Le Corbusier and Mies van der Rohe: 'I am not attracted to angles, or the straight, hard, inflexible lines created by man,' Niemeyer once said. 'I like fluid and sensual curves. The curves I find in the mountains of my homeland, in the sinuosity of its rivers, in the waves of the ocean, and on the body of a beloved woman.' The house is a sensitive integration of the spaces that are built into the heart of the canopy. The disarming simplicity of its fluid lines makes this house timeless and unique.

www.niemeyer.org.br/fundacao/locais/casa-das-canoas

The Americas      Brazil

## 05   CASA ABERTA (1968)

By Ruy Ohtake
R. Antonio de Macedo Soares, Nos. 1812, 1804, and 1800
Campo Belo, São Paulo, Brazil

**TO VISIT BEFORE YOU DIE BECAUSE**

This studio-home reveals a subtle blend of two cultural influences resulting from the architect's dual nationality.

The Japanese-Brazilian painter and sculptor Tomie Ohtake moved to Sao Paulo in 1936, where she built the studio-home of her dreams – designed by her son, the architect Ruy Ohtake (1938). The building evokes the artist's dual nationality, mixing Brazilian energy and Japanese minimalism. The Brutalist bias of the concrete sets off the artist's multicoloured works, numbered in their hundreds, that are displayed inside the house, as well as in the tropical garden. Bathed in light, the 750 m² building also includes the artist's studio, which is topped by a huge skylight – an impressive structure made of metal and glass tubes. In addition to the works of art, colour is present in the cut-out sections of wall that take on vibrant shades of blue and yellow.

No official website

The Americas — Brazil

## 06 CASA VILANOVA ARTIGAS (1949)

By João Batista Vilanova Artigas
Rua Barão de Jaceguai, 1151, Campo Belo, São Paulo, Brazil

**TO VISIT BEFORE YOU DIE BECAUSE**

Recently transformed into a cultural centre, Artigas' private home is characterised by its expressed reinforced concrete.

As godfather of the Paulista School in the 1950s, João Batista Vilanova Artigas (1915–1985) was an influential figure in Brazilian architecture. But in contrast to Niemeyer's organic formal language, this school favoured complex structures in exposed concrete, which are also typical of the work of Paulo Mendes da Rocha and Oswaldo Bratke. Artigas' 1949 home in São Paulo interweaves those Brutalist Paulista elements with international Modernist influences. 'People passing by rang the bell to ask if there was a factory, machine shop, or church,' recalls Artigas' daughter Rosa. In Artigas' time, the glass house with the atypical butterfly roof was a meeting place for communists, artists, and scientists from his left-wing entourage. After surmounting numerous obstacles, the house eventually opened to the general public in March 2019 as the Casa Vilanova Artigas Institute (ICVA): a cultural centre for architecture, design, and art, which also houses a café and co-working space. You can visit Artigas' intriguing house for free from Wednesday to Saturday. On other days, it is open by appointment only.

www.casavilanovaartigas.org

The Americas · Brazil

## 07 CASA OSCAR AMERICANO (1953)

By Oswaldo Arthur Bratke
Estrada das Canoas, No. 2310, São Conrado,
Rio de Janeiro, Brazil

**TO VISIT BEFORE YOU DIE BECAUSE**

Located in the heart of a lush tropical park, this residence encapsulates the chilled Brazilian way of life.

Oswaldo Arthur Bratke (1907–1997), who built several residences in São Paulo, was invited by his friend Oscar Americano - an engineer, patron and a successful Brazilian businessman - to build the family residence. The house has been adapted to suit the natural profile of the sloping terrain and sits proudly at the heart of a lush park, making the most of a full symbiosis with tropical nature. The entrance to the property is located in the lower part of the plot, while the house is located in the upper part, offering greater privacy. Designed along a horizontal plane in order to make the most of the gardens, the building nestles around a central patio, a kind of green oasis with tiered, cascading ponds. The Maria Luisa and Oscar Americano Foundation was created in 1974 and offers a panorama of historical and contemporary Brazil. Here you can see collections covering four centuries of paintings, porcelain, tapestries, and sacred art.

www.fundacaooscaramericano.org.br

The Americas — Brazil

## 08 CASA DE VIDRO / THE GLASS HOUSE (1951)

By Lina Bo Bardi
Rua General Almério de Moura, 200, Morumbi, São Paulo, Brazil

**TO VISIT BEFORE YOU DIE BECAUSE**

It's not every day you get to admire a tree in the heart of a modernist masterpiece in the rainforest.

The first work realised in Brazil by Lina Bo Bardi (1914–1992) was the personal residence where she and her husband were to live for 40 years. Built on *pilotis* (stilts) among the vestiges of the Mata Atlantica – the tropical rainforest surrounding São Paulo – the construction expresses the fantasy of the tree house. Though influenced by the European modernists, it is much less strict and much more sensitive. Glazed throughout and looking out onto nature, it integrates the curve and ancient references such as the turquoise mosaics of the floor – carved by hand – and a multitude of ancient objects scattered here and there. 'This residence represents an attempt to achieve a communion between nature and the natural order of things,' explained Bo Bardi. 'I have never liked the closed house that turns away from the storm and the rain, fearing all men.' Lovers of art and music, the couple hosted many artists and intellectuals, including Alexander Calder, John Cage, and Roberto Rossellini.

The Americas — Brazil

## 09 CASA WALTHER MOREIRA SALLES (1951)

By Olavo Redig de Campos – Rua Marquês de São Vicente, 476, Gávea, Rio de Janeiro, Brazil

TO VISIT BEFORE YOU DIE BECAUSE

This house offers a rare combination of Brazilian modernism with an exceptional view of the Rio mountains.

Situated on an idyllic site, surrounded by lush forest with mountains in the background, the house is a veritable modern palace. It was built by the architect Olavo Redig de Campos (1906–1984) for the family of Walther Moreira Salles, a banker, politician, and philanthropist. Set around a central courtyard with a swimming pool, it fully embodies the sensibilities of Brazilian modernism with its free, expressive forms, fully integrated within the natural environment. On the floor, the two-tone chequered marble tiles in red and white recall the architect's Italian studies at the University of Rome. Note the gigantic modules of perforated concrete that defy their original function as privacy screens and sunshades to achieve a monumental, eminently decorative character. In 1999, on the initiative of its owner, the house became the Instituto Moreira Salles, a cultural institution whose aim is to promote Brazilian culture in various fields, including photography, literature, the visual arts, and music.

www.ims.com.br

The Americas — Brazil

## 10 CASA MODERNISTA (1928)

By Gregori Warchavchik
Rua Santa Cruz, 325, Vila Mariana, São Paulo, Brazil

TO VISIT
BEFORE YOU DIE
BECAUSE

This pioneering work is considered the first example of Modernist architecture in Brazil.

This house – the former private home of the Czech-born architect Gregori Warchavchik (1896–1972) – is considered to be the first building in the Modernist spirit to appear in Brazil, and it certainly shocked the public at the time. It was also acclaimed by Warchavchik's peers, including Le Corbusier – who appointed him a delegate of the CIAM – and by members of the aristocratic intellectual elite of São Paulo who commissioned him to build numerous villas that also displayed his rigour and brutalist style. Embodying the cubist aesthetic with its assembled prisms, it is set in the middle of a 13,000 m$^2$ park that was planted by his wife Mina Klabin, a pioneer in the use of tropical species in the city. It later became the property of the municipality of São Paulo and now serves as a museum.

www.museudacidade.prefeitura.sp.gov.br/sobre-mcsp/casa-modernista/

The Americas · Canada

# 11 HABITAT 67 (1967)

By Moshe Safdie
2600 Avenue Pierre-Dupuy, Montréal,
QC H3C 3R6, Canada

**TO VISIT BEFORE YOU DIE BECAUSE**

An urban residence experience with panache, this development offers a utopian model which has never since been reproduced.

Located in the Cité du Havre – an artificial peninsula that runs alongside the river in Montréal – Habitat was the major theme exhibition of the 1967 Montréal World Exposition. As a landmark demonstration project, it pioneered a vision for urban housing using the technology of prefabricated construction. As a break-through building type that continues to resonate today, Habitat seeks to create a vital neighbourhood with open spaces, garden terraces, and many other amenities typically reserved for the single-family home, now adapted to a high-density city environment.

The innovative concept is based on the assembly of 365 prefabricated cubic modules in concrete, connected to create 158 residences. These range in size from 56 m² one-bedroom dwellings to 170 m² four-bedroom dwellings. In all, there are 15 different housing types. The composition of stepped modules provides every dwelling with access to sun and air, as well as a private garden terrace. Play areas for young children are provided throughout the building. Over the course of the last fifty years, residents have been able to modify and combine some of the modules, working to balance individual interests and needs with the desire to preserve the complex and respect its status as a National Heritage Building in Canada.

www.habitat67.com

The Americas    Mexico

# 12 CASA BARRAGÁN (1948)

By Luis Barragán
General Francisco Ramírez 12-14,
Colonia Ampliación Daniel Garza, CP 11840, Mexico City, Mexico

TO VISIT BEFORE YOU DIE BECAUSE

See how colour and light bring a spiritual atmosphere to the studio-home of Luis Barragán.

Luis Barragán (1902–1988) built his house on the outskirts of Mexico City. As soon as you enter the building, you are in touch with the Barragán style: the hall is covered with a black floor that contrasts with the fuchsia pink walls. There is a predominance of colour, with a palette that is both bright and soft, composed of pink, yellow, orange, and terracotta. The only colour absent from his work is green, because the architect believed it to be a colour found in nature. Passionate about horses, and both classical and African music, he surrounded himself with many objects that evoked his passions, such as record players, which are placed here and there around the building. Barragán designed or chose every piece of furniture and object in the building's interior, most of which were brought back from his many travels in Europe and Africa. Several of Joseph Albers' 'homages to the square' recall his love of colour and geometry. A religious man, he divided the shutters of his windows into four wooden sections, so the sunlight passing through them would form the shape of a cross.

The Americas · Mexico

# 13 CASA AZUL / THE BLUE HOUSE (1904)

By Guillermo Kahlo
Londres 247, Colonia del Carmen, Delegación Coyoacán, CP 04100, Mexico City, Mexico

TO VISIT BEFORE YOU DIE BECAUSE

This house offers a moving and intimate dive into the deep blue depths of Frida Kahlo's world.

From the outside, the house would hardly be noticeable if its walls were not painted blue. Built by her father, this is the house in which Frida Kahlo was born and where she lived for most of her life – at times with her husband Diego Rivera. The artist's spirit is present in every corner of the house as well as in the beautiful patio and the gardens lined with cacti and exotic plants. Now a museum, the house contains some of her works, books, and other personal objects - such as the pre-Columbian statuettes that she collected by the thousand. Above the bed is a mirror on the ceiling where Frida, confined to bed after her dramatic accident in which a bus crash injured her spine and pelvis and broke her collarbone, two ribs, and her leg, was able to see herself as she painted her self-portrait. On the walls of the room, three portraits of Lenin, Stalin, and Mao reveal her political convictions. The house hosted Trotsky during his Mexican exile in 1937, and it was at this time that all the façades of the house were painted blue. The sunny kitchen reflects the couple's shared passion for traditional Mexican cuisine. It is here that they received their guests, including many artists and intellectuals.

www.museofridakahlo.org.mx/en/the-blue-house/

The Americas · Mexico

## 14 CASA ESTUDIO DIEGO RIVERA Y FRIDA KAHLO (1931)

By Juan O'Gorman
Diego Rivera 2, Altavista Corner, San Ángel Inn,
Álvaro Obregón, CP 01060, Mexico City, Mexico

TO VISIT BEFORE YOU DIE BECAUSE

This house embodies the love–hate relationship of two of the greatest artists of the 20th century.

This is one of the first creation realised by the Modern movement in Latin America, consisting of two pavilions that take into account the Corbusian precepts emerging from Europe. The complex was built by Juan O'Gorman (1905–1982), a painter and architect and a friend of Diego Rivera. Frida had the blue house, Diego had the white, and they lived there for only a short time. Frida left Diego and moved into the Casa Azul, where she had grown up as a child and a young woman. Despite their subsequent reconciliation, the couple decided to live separately. The houses have sawtooth roofs and are connected by a suspended walkway. They are surrounded by an enclosure made of cacti, which creates a discreet boundary between the interior and exterior. Along with their modernity, they also preserve the traditions of Mexican culture, most notably through the colourful murals and the rows of cacti. They have now been turned into a museum featuring many works by the artist couple, including a superb collection of papier-mâché figures by Diego Rivera depicting humans, skeletons, and animals.

The Americas · Mexico

## 15 CASA O'GORMAN (1929)

By Juan O'Gorman
San Ángel Inn, Álvaro Obregón, Mexico City, Mexico

TO VISIT
BEFORE YOU DIE
BECAUSE

Frida Kahlo's neighbour wrote architectural history when he created this functionalist private residence.

The Irish-Mexican artist-architect Juan O'Gorman (1905-1982) was barely 24 years old when he designed this home in 1929. It is the first and most important functionalist home in all of Latin America. The kinship with Le Corbusier's Villa Savoye, which was built almost simultaneously, is compelling. This is hardly surprising because, as a student, O'Gorman received a copy of Le Corbusier's book *Vers Une Architecture*, which shaped his architectural approach. Yet this concrete house on stilts with its characteristic spiral staircase also displays typical South American features: just think of the funky cactus hedge and the brick-red window frames. O'Gorman's design philosophy ran a similar course to that of Le Corbusier: he renounced 'machine-inspired' modernism and evolved into a more organic visual language. Apart from that, the house also made history through its famous neighbours: Diego Rivera and Frida Kahlo. Rivera was so impressed by O'Gorman's design that, in 1931, he commissioned him to build a double studio house on the plot next door for himself and Kahlo.

No official website

The Americas — Mexico

# 16 CASA ORGÁNICA (1984)

By Javier Senosiain
Acueducto Morelia 6, Vista del Valle, 53296 Naucalpan de Juárez, State of Mexico, Mexico

**TO VISIT BEFORE YOU DIE BECAUSE**

This building stands as a true embodiment of the relationship between humans and nature.

The Mexican architect Javier Senosiain (1948), a supporter of bio-architecture, proposed a particular approach for this house, with its free, moving forms inspired by nature. Each space is designed to integrate the human form as much as possible, without taking into account the usual presumptions of what a house is supposed to look like. Strongly influenced by Gaudi, Senosiain designed a phantasmagorical interior, made of caves, tubular corridors, and curved tunnels, almost enough to make you go dizzy. The walls are made of ferro-cement sprayed onto metal armatures. Semi-buried underground, the house is completely covered with vegetation that helps it blend into the landscape, protects it from the sun, and restricts variations in temperature. Facing south to capture the sun, the windows, which serve as veritable paintings of the surrounding nature, are positioned in the places overlooking the loveliest parts of the garden. The earth and the sun have a complementary role in maintaining a stable temperature inside the house: the earth protects the inhabitants from the hot and the cold, while the sun keeps the premises warm and bright.

www.arquitecturaorganica.com/habitat/la-casa-organica

The Americas — USA

# 17 ALAN I W FRANK HOUSE (1940)

By Walter Gropius and Marcel Breuer
96 East Woodland Road, Pittsburgh, PA 15232, USA

**TO VISIT BEFORE YOU DIE BECAUSE**

This is a veritable masterpiece in the integration of architecture, furnishings, and landscape.

The Frank House was built as a large family home for Cecelia and Robert Frank, Pittsburgh industrialists who were receptive to modern ideas and new forms of architecture. It was following a conference in Pittsburgh led by the founder of the Bauhaus, Walter Gropius (1883–1969), that they decided to choose him to build their house. Gropius teamed up with Marcel Breuer (1902–1981) and together they went on to build a huge residence on four levels with five terraces, nine bedrooms, and thirteen bathrooms (!) – all set off by an indoor swimming pool and a dancefloor on the roof. Inside, graceful curves prevail, alongside luxurious materials and meticulous detailing. The walls are covered with pearwood, sycamore, redwood, travertine, and stone. The spectacular glass-brick entrance and the impressive cantilevered staircase give this 'machine for living' a modern and comfortable atmosphere for the whole family.

www.thefrankhouse.org

The Americas  USA

# 18 ALDEN B. DOW HOME AND STUDIO (1934–1941)

By Alden B. Dow
315 Post St, Midland, Michigan, MI 48640, USA

TO VISIT BEFORE YOU DIE BECAUSE

Gardens never end and buildings never begin.

Midland in Michigan, about 130 kilometres from Detroit, is an under-the-radar hotspot for mid-century architecture in the States. One of the first to see the potential of the place was Alden B. Dow (1904-1983), the son of Herbert Henry Dow: the founder of the Dow chemical concern. Alden graduated in 1931 as an architect from Colombia University. In 1933, he spent a year with Frank Lloyd Wright in Taliesin, and the following year he started his own office. His first major completed project was his own studio-home, which remains a perfect illustration of his organic design credo: 'Gardens never end and buildings never begin.' Of course, the studio home bears the stamp of Wright, particularly in the way that the landscape, water features and architecture interweave. Despite the whimsical overhanging roofs, the striking colour palette, the numerous geometric motifs, and the stacked building blocks, the 'cubist' house exudes tranquillity and a sense of the organic. A fact that wasn't lost on the jury of the Paris Exposition Internationale des Arts et Techniques dans la Vie Moderne (1937): Dow won the first prize there. Fancy a visit? Reservations are require

www.abdow.org

The Americas USA

# 19 JUDD FOUNDATION (1972–1994)

By Donald Judd
104 South Highland Avenue, Marfa, Texas,
TX 79843-0218, USA

TO VISIT
BEFORE YOU DIE
BECAUSE

Judd transformed a former military base and buildings in the desert town into a singular place for the permanent installation of art.

Donald Judd's (1928 - 1994) New York loft in SoHo is not the only place in the world where you can dive so deeply into his universe. In 1971, disenchanted by the commodification of New York's art scene, he sought seclusion in Marfa, a small desert town in far West Texas near the Mexican border. Over the years, he purchased various buildings, including a former hotel, a bank, a grocery store and airplane hangars of the military base, which he transformed to suit his own ideas for the installation of art. La Mansana de Chinati, also known as the Block, is a complex of buildings which houses his art collection, private home, libraries and studios. Later, with the initial help of the Dia Art Foundation, he established the site at the former Fort D.A. Russell military base as an exhibition space for large-scale work. For Judd, the landscape in and around Marfa became a space central to his ideas on preservation. Over the years, Marfa has attained a kind of utopian pilgrimage status for Judd aficionados willing to brave a cinematic road trip to visit an arid corner of the States.

www.juddfoundation.org/visit/marfa/

The Americas  USA

## 20  EAMES HOUSE (1949)

By Charles and Ray Eames
203 N. Chautauqua Blvd. Pacific Palisades, California, CA 90272, USA

---

TO VISIT BEFORE YOU DIE BECAUSE

Of all the prefab homes of the Case Study Houses, this is the most personal.

The Eames House is part of the Case Study programme: an initiative of the magazine *Arts & Architecture*. Publisher John Entenza challenged architects to design a series of experimental houses in California that were affordable and easily duplicable in post-war America. Among all the Case Study Houses, the Charles and Ray Eames dwelling occupies a special place. Because their first L-shaped design looked a little too much like a Van der Rohe home, the couple started again. In 1949, they designed a prefabricated quick-build house in steel, with a Mondrian-esque exterior and Japanese-influenced interior. Inside, the home is an unusually airy series of spaces, some of which are intimate, some double height. With its inventive off-the-shelf elements - the steel construction was erected within a day and a half! - and its relationship to nature, the Eames House set the standard for post-war modern living in the States. Charles (1907 - 1978) and Ray Eames (1912 - 1988) lived here until the end of their life.

www.eamesfoundation.org/house/eames-house

The Americas  USA

# 21 ELROD HOUSE (1968)

By John Lautner
2175 Southridge Drive, Palm Springs, California, CA 92264, USA

**TO VISIT BEFORE YOU DIE BECAUSE**

Play a Bond villain in this work of organic architecture which was used as a set for a lair in the film *Diamonds are Forever*.

Built on the side of a mountain for the interior designer Arthur Elrod, the house displays all the characteristics of John Lautner's (1911 - 1994) constructions: built on difficult terrain, with a modest entrance, an extravagant interior, and with only a fine line between interior and exterior. Like some kind of modern take on a cave, it belongs to the current of organic architecture, with mountain rocks in the heart of the living room and an 'infinite' swimming pool flowing from the indoor/out-outdoor space to the pavilion patio edge, where it falls to the canyon hillside below. The conical roof that allows the light to pass through is certainly its most original component. The living room has a superb panoramic view of Mount San Jacinto, Mount San Gorgonio, and the Palm Springs Valley. In 1971, the house was used as the lair of a James Bond villain in the film *Diamonds are Forever*.

The Americas — USA

# 22 FALLINGWATER HOUSE (1936–1939)

By Frank Lloyd Wright
1491 Mill Run Road, Mill Run, Pennsylvania, PA 15464, USA

**TO VISIT BEFORE YOU DIE BECAUSE**

This is a *tour de force* of organic architecture and one of the most famous houses in the world.

It's the embodiment of a dream, the fantasy of living on a waterfall. Frank Lloyd Wright (1867–1959) revolutionised housing design by creating an avant-garde ecological model for the businessman Edgar Jonas Kaufmann. Located on the banks of Bear Run River in Pennsylvania, the house achieves a perfect symbiosis with nature and preserves its wild character. It extends from a vertical tower of natural stone that is the hub for a series of cantilevered concrete terraces. These play the dual role of serving as observation points from which to witness the natural environment, as well as acoustic screens to soften the sounds of the waterfall. Nature enters on all sides, thanks to the large bay windows and glass ceilings, which frame the views of the water and the surrounding vegetation. This is a perfectly realised work of organic architecture, in which Wright mixes traditional and modern materials, sensitivity, and refinement, to produce a sustainable form of architecture, an inexhaustible source of inspiration for the new generation.

www.fallingwater.org

The Americas — USA

## 23 FARNSWORTH HOUSE (1946–1951)

By Ludwig Mies van der Rohe
14520 River Rd Gate 1, Plano, Illinois, IL 60545, USA

**TO VISIT BEFORE YOU DIE BECAUSE**

Experience a sense of weightlessness in a house at the heart of nature.

Despite the great serenity that emanates from the house, it was the subject of a litigious dispute between its architect Mies van der Rohe (1886 - 1969) and his client Edith Farnsworth, a kidney specialist. She dreamt of a modern second home where she could devote herself to her passions: nature, the violin, and the translation of poetry. Mies van der Rohe designed a variation on the Barcelona Pavilion that he built in 1929, entirely glazed, and with a free plan. It is composed of two horizontal slabs that form the floor and the roof. Following the example of Philip Johnson's Glass House, the extensive use of glass turns the house into an observatory for the natural environment and pushes its symbiosis with nature to the very limit. Located in a flood zone, it is raised 1.50 metres off the ground and seems to float above the land it occupies. The conflict between the architect and his client ultimately led to an unfinished project, with the furniture eventually fitted out by one of Mies van der Rohe's students.

www.farnsworthhouse.org

The Americas — USA

## 24 FRANK LLOYD WRIGHT HOUSE / THE KRAUS HOUSE (1952)

By Frank Lloyd Wright
120 North Ballas Rd, Kirkwood, Missouri, MO 63122, USA

**TO VISIT BEFORE YOU DIE BECAUSE**

This is a supreme example of Wright's Usonian architecture: simple, stylish, and affordable.

Nestled in a field in Missouri, the Kraus House is an excellent example of Wright's (1867 - 1959) democratic vision of providing middle-class Americans with beautiful architecture at an affordable price. Built for Russell and Ruth Kraus, its highly expressive forms give the house the appearance of a sculpture. Considered to be one of Wright's most geometrically complex houses, it is composed of two interlocking parallelograms and is built around an open plan with a central foyer. The main terrace doors include stained-glass windows designed by Russell Kraus, who was himself an artist working in mosaics and stained glass. The house is remarkable not only for its architectural integrity, but also for its original furniture and fabrics, which were designed entirely by Wright.

www.ebsworthpark.org

The Americas  USA

## 25 FRANK SINATRA HOUSE (1947)

By E. Stewart Williams
1148 East Alejo Road, Palm Springs, California, CA 92262, USA

TO VISIT
BEFORE YOU DIE
BECAUSE

Host an epic pool party against the backdrop of Sinatra's piano-shaped swimming pool.

Did you know that Frank Sinatra really was a desert rat? The American crooner was one of the first stars to purchase a villa in Palm Springs, the sophisticated desert town in California that saw an exuberant surge in property development after World War II. Legend has it that on 1 May 1947 – holding an ice cream and wearing a sailor cap – Sinatra walked into the Williams, Williams & Williams office in Palm Springs and asked for a 'house that would be ready by Christmas'. Architect E. Stewart Williams (1909 - 2005) had barely seven months, but with a budget of US$150,000 he thought he'd give it a try. Sinatra actually wanted a 'Georgian style' mansion, but Williams persuaded him to agree to a sleek Modernist villa with panoramic views. Sinatra lived there from Christmas 1948 to 1957, when he had another house built a little further away in Palm Springs. The heavy partying and domestic drama in his 'Twin Palms' villa are witnessed by the cracked hand basin: in a drunken temper, the singer allegedly threw a bottle of champagne at his current wife Ava Gardner. Although the villa has been renovated, none of the era's 'star allure' has been lost: who wouldn't want to host a party around the original piano-shaped swimming pool? If you're planning a glamorous event, this is the perfect backdrop. Architecture-lovers can even hire the villa for a sleepover, although it comes with a hefty price tag: US$2200 a night. A cheaper option is to join a Mid Century Home Tour in Palm Springs: a mecca for lovers of what has been dubbed 'desert modernism'.

www.sinatrahouse.com

The Americas    USA

# 26 FREDERICK C. ROBIE HOUSE (1910)

By Frank Lloyd Wright
5757 S. Woodlawn Avenue, Chicago, Illinois, IL 60637, USA

**TO VISIT BEFORE YOU DIE BECAUSE**

Frank Lloyd Wright's first masterpiece showcases the first architectural style considered uniquely American.

Until the early 20th century, North America had no architectural style of which to speak. But all that changed with the emergence of the Prairie School, then known as the Chicago School. The Robie House (built between 1909 and 1910), which has been on the UNESCO World Heritage List since July 2019, is the best example of the Prairie School. The 28-year-old businessman Frederick C. Robie wanted 'as modern a home as possible', so Frank Lloyd Wright (1867 - 1959) came up with a totally new design, conceived as two squared rectangles. The low terraces and generous canopies give the building its typical horizontality, reminiscent of the vast Midwest landscape in which Wright grew up. Robie lived there for only 14 months. The architectural gem was scheduled for demolition but was saved at the last minute by fierce campaigning.

## 27 FREY HOUSE II (1964)

By Albert Frey
686 Palisades Drive, Palm Springs, California, CA 92262, USA

TO VISIT
BEFORE YOU DIE
BECAUSE

This extraordinary house offers a spectacular view of the city and the desert.

Albert Frey (1903–1998) played a major role in modern American architecture and is credited with inventing desert modernism. He chose the desert of Palm Springs to serve as the backdrop for his second residence. A veritable belvedere that opens out onto the impressive Thaquitz Canyon, it is built on the side of a mountain, perched where no one would ever have imagined building. It is the power of the rock – which is welcomed into the very heart of the house – that provides its brutal beauty. Frey created a house covering 90 m$^2$, entirely glazed and extremely modest, which stands out in contrast to the stunning landscape. In its location and simplicity, it recalls the wooden shed created by his mentor, Le Corbusier. Below, a concrete swimming pool in the shape of a raindrop blends in with the mountain rock. Visits to the house offer the promise of a journey into the world of the architect and are led by the historian Michael Stern, who knew Albert Frey.

## 28 GAMBLE HOUSE (1908)

By Greene & Greene
4 Westmoreland Place, Pasadena, California, CA 91103, California, USA

TO VISIT
BEFORE YOU DIE
BECAUSE

America's best-preserved Arts and Crafts style villa belonged to the son of the founder of Procter & Gamble.

The architects Charles (1868–1957) and Henry (1870 - 1954) Green received from their clients Mary and David Gamble - son of the co-founder of multinational Procter & Gamble – a big budget to design a winter residence in Pasadena. With its extraordinarily detailed bespoke work and astonishing craftsmanship, Gamble House is the best-preserved masterpiece in the Arts and Crafts style in America. The interiors with stained-glass windows by Emil Lange and bespoke features in no fewer than 17 types of wood have lost none of their lustre. As a cross between a Japanese *ryokan* and a Swiss mountain cabin, the house seems rooted in tradition. But inside it is equipped with all the 'mod cons', from electric lighting to intercoms. When David Gamble's heirs planned to sell the house in 1944, they discovered, in the nick of time, that the prospective buyer disliked the dark wood interior and was planning to paint it white once the sale was completed. The Gambles were so upset that they decided to donate the house to the University of Southern California School of Architecture. They still organise guided tours of the house.

The Americas USA

## 29 GARCIA HOUSE (1962)

By John Lautner
Mulholland Drive, Hollywood Hills, Los Angeles, California, USA

TO VISIT
BEFORE YOU DIE
BECAUSE

Witness the genuinely unique shape of this 'rainbow house'.

This incredible eye-shaped belvedere offers a breathtaking view of the canyon. Once again, John Lautner (1911 - 1994) offers a very sensual and spectacular form of architecture, based on curves and the marriage of natural and industrial materials. The current owners, John McIlwee and Bill Damaschke, have restored Garcia House to its former glory following a meticulous restoration. The slender structure is perched on two high, V-shaped pillars, a form that is characteristic of the sixties. As they look out onto nature, the façades of the 'eye' are entirely glazed, using a geometric arrangement of transparent and coloured panels. An imposing chimney made of lava stone breaks the curve and provides a powerful contrast of materials. Inside, several original layouts have been preserved, such as the planters and the lounge seating, but these have been mixed with modern elements for a perfectly executed retro-contemporary blend.

## 30 GHOST RANCH (1948)

By Georgia O'Keeffe
280 Private Drive 1708, Highway 84, Abiquiú, New Mexico, NM 87510, USA

TO VISIT
BEFORE YOU DIE
BECAUSE

See the house that earned O'Keeffe the sobriquet 'mother of American modernism'.

The American artist Georgia O'Keeffe (1887-1986) loved nothing more than driving alone through the desert landscape of New Mexico. Cruising past haciendas, rocks, and ranches, she was able to escape her life in New York, a city that literally made her depressed. In Abiquiú her eye fell on a dilapidated Spanish colonial villa, but for ten years the owner – the Catholic Church – refused to sell it to her. When she was finally able to acquire the hacienda in 1945, she spent three years remodelling it so radically that the artist was immediately christened 'the mother of American modernism'. It is fantastic to see how the colours and textures of her studio-home in adobe – a mixture of manure, straw, sand, water, and clay – almost become one with the dramatic landscape. Visitors who take a guided tour of the remote dwelling are touched not only by her powerful paintings and extraordinary life but, most notably, by the way in which she left her modernist mark on the cinematic landscape.

www.johnlautner.org   www.ghostranch.org

The Americas  USA

## 31 GRACE MILLER HOUSE (1937)

By Richard Neutra
2311 North Indian Canyon Drive, Palm Springs, California, CA 92262, USA

**TO VISIT BEFORE YOU DIE BECAUSE**

One of Neutra's most important creations, this house prioritises customisation and wellbeing.

This is certainly one of the finest examples of a good understanding between an architect, Richard Neutra (1892–1970), and his client, Grace Miller, both of whom were convinced that a well-designed house can have a positive effect on the physical and mental health of its inhabitants. The project was to design a winter home and studio for the gymnastic exercise that Grace Miller was teaching. Over the course of the project, they exchanged an extensive correspondence of more than fifty letters in which the client shared the details of her daily lifestyle. Even with the limited budget of $7500 it was possible to build an extremely personalised home, with every detail tailored to Mrs Miller's specific needs. The sense of serenity clearly reflects the influences of the Japanese tea houses that Neutra had visited during his trip in 1930. To get the full experience, you can also rent the house for the night, or maybe more…

## 32 THE GLASS HOUSE (1950)

By Philip Johnson
199 Elm St, New Canaan, Connecticut, CT 06840, USA

**TO VISIT BEFORE YOU DIE BECAUSE**

The Glass House is considered to be the most influential house of the 20th century.

The ultimate glass house, designed in 1950 by Philip Johnson (1906-2005), has been cited countless times in architectural textbooks. Johnson was a highly influential figure, appointed the first head of the architecture department at the New York Museum of Modern Art (MOMA). With exhibitions such as International Style (1932), he introduced Mies van der Rohe to the American public. The Glass House is a lucid expression of Mies' inspiration. Idyllically situated in the wooded area of New Canaan, Connecticut, it is a flawless box of steel and glass. Within this transparent lookout post nestling in a wooded domain, privacy is reduced to zero. Seeking an abode that offered an unimpeded view of nature, Johnson composed an entirely open structure, where the living areas are delineated solely by furniture or other interior elements. This Bauhaus-influenced house is undoubtedly the zenith of residential architecture, but Johnson's architectural style continued to evolve. This is soon apparent when you visit the Glass House: Johnson added pavilions and sculptural details to the grounds, but fortunately these don't compromise the integrity of the house.

www.arrivednow.com/RichardNeutraDesignedGraceMillerHouse/

www.theglasshouse.org

The Americas                    USA

# 33  GROPIUS HOUSE (1938)

By Walter Gropius
68 Baker Bridge Road #3105, Lincoln, Massachusetts,
MA 01773, USA

TO VISIT
BEFORE YOU DIE
BECAUSE

Gropius' first commissioned residential project in the States gives equal emphasis to architectural integrity and decorative arts.

Gropius' own home in Lincoln, Massachusetts, is part of the canon of international modernism. His house is a fusion of the regional architecture tradition in New England, mixed with his contemporary design philosophy. Walter Gropius (1883 - 1969), who founded the Bauhaus in 1919, fled from Nazi Germany in 1934 and arrived in America via a detour to Great Britain in 1937. A year later he built his own family home there, according to the principles of the Bauhaus: a house as a functional machine, carefully designed to maximise efficiency, built of industrial materials and with a practical, open layout. Although the design was not America's first acquaintance with the European modernist's work, the roof terrace, glass block wall, and striking entrance pavilion would prove to be particularly influential. In 1932, architect Philip Johnson had already selected him as one of 'four pioneers of modern architecture' in his influential exhibition Modern Architecture: International Exhibition at MoMa, New York, along with Le Corbusier, Mies van der Rohe, and J.J.P. Oud.

www.historicnewengland.org/property/gropius-house

The Americas — USA

# 34 HOLLYHOCK HOUSE (1919–1921)

By Frank Lloyd Wright
4800 Hollywood Blvd, Los Angeles, California, CA 90027, USA

**TO VISIT BEFORE YOU DIE BECAUSE**

Succumb to the allure of a Mayan temple in this creation, named after its resident's favourite flower.

Originally designed by Frank Lloyd Wright (1867 - 1959) as the home for the oil heiress Aline Barnsdall, Hollyhock House was intended to form part of an artistic and theatrical complex, but the project was never brought to completion. At the time, Wright was away on the construction site of the Imperial Hotel in Japan and was unable to supervise the building site in person, a task that he entrusted to his son Lloyd and to his assistant Rudolph Schindler. The complex takes on the astonishing appearance of a Mayan temple, with its exterior façades inclined at an angle of 85° and the many sculptures and acroteria based on the motif of the stylised hollyhocks that give the house its name. It is arranged around a central courtyard, one side of which is open to form a kind of theatrical stage with a pool. It was in this house that Wright experimented with mitred-glass windows, which he was to use again in his design for Fallingwater.

www.franklloydwright.org/site/hollyhock-house

The Americas — USA

## 35 JAMES ROSE CENTER (1953)

By James Rose
506 East Ridgewood Avenue, Ridgewood, New Jersey, NJ 07450, USA

**TO VISIT BEFORE YOU DIE BECAUSE**

Like all living things, this house is in a state of perpetual evolution; its design grows, matures, and renews itself.

Built by and for the landscape architect James Rose (1913–1991), the house is inspired by traditional Asian culture and American design. Consisting of three buildings – with a primary home for his mother, a guesthouse for his sister, and a studio for himself - it preserves the site where it took root, a former tram stop. Between architecture and landscape, between interior and exterior, this unique place is transformed, like nature, by the seasons and the passage of time. The extensive use of wood allows the spaces to be fully integrated with the nature that surrounds them. By the time Rose died in 1991, the property had largely deteriorated and some of his friends began restoring it in order to reconvert it into a centre for research and landscape studies, thus fulfilling the architect's wish: to design a place in constant metamorphosis.

www.jamesrosecenter.org/

The Americas — USA

# 36 KENTUCK KNOB (1956)

By Frank Lloyd Wright
723 Kentuck Rd, Dunbar, Pennsylvania, PA 15431, USA

**TO VISIT BEFORE YOU DIE BECAUSE**

This hexagonal, one-storey Usonian house is perfectly integrated with the landscape.

This was one of the last houses designed by Frank Lloyd Wright (1867 - 1959). He was 89 years old and was working hard at the time on the Guggenheim Museum in New York. The Hagans had fallen in love with Fallingwater, which was home to their friends the Kaufmanns, so it was only natural that they should turn to Wright for their own design. Kentuck Knob is one of his Usonian houses, in which he uses vernacular materials such as native sandstone and red cypress in the beautiful details that can be seen, for example, on the skylight canopy over the porch. Built in the mountains above Uniontown in western Pennsylvania, the construction blends into its natural surroundings. The Hagans sold their home in 1986 to the Englishman Lord Peter Palumbo, who opened the house to the public and incorporated a collection of thirty or so sculptures of modern and contemporary art around the house, including a piece of the Berlin Wall and sculptures by Andy Goldsworthy, Claes Oldenburg, and Sir Anthony Caro.

www.kentuckknob.com/

The Americas     USA

# 37 KORMAN HOUSE (1971–1973)

By Louis Kahn
Fort Washington, Philadelphia, PA, USA

**TO VISIT BEFORE YOU DIE BECAUSE**

This house represents Kahn's unconventional and enduring vision of the American country home.

Real estate developers Steven and Toby Korman asked Louis Kahn (1901–1974) to design a house. The American architect had turned down the contract several times, but eventually agreed. It was to be Kahn's last residential project: in march 1974, he died in the men's bathroom at Penn station after returning from Bangladesh. Before leaving for that trip, Kahn and his wife Esther had dinner at this house. That night, he even positioned the art and played Mozart on the piano. Kahn mostly designed monumental public buildings, and in the end, fewer than nine of the private residences he designed were actually built. 'I would say a house is a society of spaces talking to each other, expressing a way of life,' he said in 1972, when he was working on Korman House. Kahn's largest private residence in Fort Washington is the perfect reflection of his philosophy of living and monumental style. The interior has since been reinterpreted by New Yorker Jennifer Post, but the volumes and play of light are still classic Kahn. If you visit the house, you'll discover how the architect applied his ideas with great consistency throughout this contemporary American villa. His use of materials is subtle and refined, with the minimum of detail. Louis Kahn added a lot of built-in furnishings: the staircase alone was three months in the making. Kahn's scenography of light and space is tightly structured and disciplined. Unfortunately, the mansion is currently not accepting visitors.

www.kahnkormanhouse.com

The Americas — USA

# 38 LILJESTRAND HOUSE (1952)

By Vladimir Ossipoff
3300 Tantalus Drive, Honolulu, Hawaii, HI 96822, USA

**TO VISIT BEFORE YOU DIE BECAUSE**

Respecting its location, this house has been seamlessly adapted to the lush topography and microclimates of the island.

Located on the slopes of Mount Tantalus overlooking Honolulu, the Liljestrand House is an outstanding example of the work of Vladimir Ossipoff (1907–1998), an architect recognised as the master of modern architecture in Hawaii. The clients, Howard (a doctor) and Betty Liljestrand, intended to design their house themselves, but they soon changed their minds and hired an architect with whom they collaborated throughout the course of the project. With lots of sun, rain, and wind, Hawaii's highly variable weather conditions imposed construction constraints. The house is laid out on two levels, with the upper part sheltered from the frequent mountain showers, while the louvred wooden shutters of the windows filter a refreshing breeze. The house has been fully integrated into its environment, with the master bedroom set at an angle to preserve an ancestral eucalyptus tree. The lower floor opens out onto the terrace, while the pool down below offers a breathtaking view of the island. Ossipoff has synthesised influences from East and West, including Japanese construction techniques and modern architectural principles.

www.liljestrandhouse.org

The Americas — USA

# 39 MANITOGA (1942–1961)

By Russel Wright
584 NY-Route 9D, Garrison, New York, NY 10524, USA

**TO VISIT BEFORE YOU DIE BECAUSE**

Russel Wright flooded a quarry just so he could live by the water in this house whose name means 'place of great spirit'.

'I would like to create a shelter in which I can enjoy the beauty of this land, the woods, the stones, the sky, the river, the animals. I do not want this house to dominate the country,' said industrial designer Russel Wright (1904-1976) of his Manitoga studio-home in Garrison, New York. The location of the house alone is unique. In 1942, Russel and his wife chose a piece of land verging on a disused quarry. He redirected a mountain stream to fill it with water. By integrating green roofs and using a cedar trunk as a supporting column, he blurs the boundary between inside and outside. The house has a distinctive Japanese sensibility, thanks to the involvement in the design of architect David Leavitt (1918-2013). He had earned his stripes in Japan in Antonin Raymond's office. Natural materials take pride of place both in the home and the studio, but Wright also experimented with synthetic materials, such as combining butterfly wings with transparent plastic and integrating pine needles in plaster walls. It is this playful juxtaposition of the natural and manmade that makes the place so irresistible.

www.visitmanitoga.org

The Americas    USA

# 40 BERNARD SCHWARTZ HOUSE / STILL BEND (1939)

By Frank Lloyd Wright
Still Bend, PO Box 165, Two Rivers, Wisconsin, USA

TO VISIT
BEFORE YOU DIE
BECAUSE

It is one of the only Frank Lloyd Wright houses you can rent.

In 1938, even before the Case Study Programme, Life Magazine launched their project 'Eight Houses for Modern Living'. In collaboration with The Architectural Forum, architects such as Frank Lloyd Wright were invited to design a dream house for four types of American families, based on their average incomes. Frank Lloyd Wright designed a usonian house for the Blackbournes, who earned around 5500 dollar. Unfortunately, the middle-class family never built Wright's design. However, Bernard Schwartz, a business man from Two Rivers, Wisconsin, got to know the project and met Wright in Taliesin to realise his Life Magazine design. Using cypress wood and bricks, the architect slightly adapted the materials and heightened the ceiling in the living area. He even designed furniture and home accessories for the house, that were not part of Life Magazine's initial pitch. Wright named the residence 'Still Bend' and Bernard and Fern Schwartz lived there until 1971. Since 2003 the house is owned by Gary and Michael Ditmer, who restored it and made it available for rent to the public. You can experience the house for 475 – 750 dollar a night, depending on season and availability. Guests can enjoy the natural flow of Wright's design, and discover how he translated the horizontality of the river landscape into a cosy family home.

www.theschwartzhouse.com/

The Americas  USA

# 41 MILLER HOUSE (1953)

By Eero Saarinen
506 5th Street, Columbus, Indiana, IN 47201, USA

TO VISIT BEFORE YOU DIE BECAUSE

A combination of the open planning, interior design, and landscape architecture equip this house with a simple serenity.

This residence was commissioned by the industrialist and architectural patron J. Irwin Miller and his wife Xenia. It is one of the few single-family houses designed by Eero Saarinen (1910–1961). It fully embodies the modern architectural tradition with its open and fluid plan; its flat roof; and the choice of glass, metal, and stone as its materials. Outside, the attention is drawn to an astonishing skylight structure supported by 16 cruciform steel columns, creating plays of light and shade. Inside, the atmosphere invites contemplation, with a 15-metre long library, a suspended cylindrical chimney, and a cosy, semi-enclosed meeting room. The dining room is furnished with Saarinen's famous 'Tulip' range. On the façade, two Japanese cherry trees frame the entrance and complete the quiet flatness of the house. After the death of the Miller couple, their heirs generously donated the house to the Indianapolis Museum of Art.

www.columbus.in.us/miller-house-and-garden-tour

The Americas · USA

## 42 THE MODULIGHTOR BUILDING (1989)

By Paul Rudolph
246 East 58th Street, New York, NY 10022, USA

**TO VISIT BEFORE YOU DIE BECAUSE**

Take the opportunity to see New York's only Paul Rudolph interior which is visitable.

When asked if he made his architecture too complex, Paul Rudolph (1918-1997) invariably answered: 'Architecture is like music. Do you think a Bach fugue is too complicated?' Typical of Rudolph and the Modulightor Building in New York, one of his last achievements, is the geometric façade: it is composed of a stack of rectangles and squares, which seems independent of the subdivision into storeys. The history of the project dates back to 1989, when Rudolph designed a complex narrow 8-storey building entirely in steel, concrete, and glass. Initially, the first four floors were finished. He reserved the second floor for his office. Floors 3 and 4 were rental apartments. After his death in 1997, one of his most loyal employees converted the two duplexes into one large sculptural apartment that you can pre-book to visit on the first Friday of every month. There you will see the conceptual evolution of Rudolph's layered architecture, his use of vertical and horizontal elements to create dynamics, why he was so infatuated with modular furniture, and what he collected.

www.paulrudolphheritagefoundation.org/1989modulightor

The Americas — USA

# 43 HARVEY HOUSE (1950)

By John Lautner
2180 West Live Oak Drive, Los Angeles, California, USA

TO VISIT BEFORE YOU DIE BECAUSE

The multiple use of the circular form lends this house an impression of infinity.

Leo Harvey was a wealthy industrialist who made his money in aluminium. Architect John Lautner (1911 - 1994) designed this remarkable house for Harvey and his wife in 1950. It is built around a concentric layout and offers 360° panoramic views of the surrounding natural area. The form of the circle is repeated in different forms in a range of mutually responsive materials, incorporating wood, natural stone, and concrete in a particularly harmonious blend. Outside, a curved swimming pool hugs the rounded shape of the building also. The house was recently restored by the architect Helena Arahuete, who was herself part of Lautner's office. Arahuete managed to restore its original layout, while also meeting the needs and tastes of the current owners, the actress Kelly Lynch and her husband Mitch Glazer – who sometimes hold chamber music concerts here that offer a wonderful opportunity to discover the house.

The Americas — USA

## 44 NEUTRA VDL HOUSE (1932)

By Richard Neutra
2300 Silver Lake Boulevard, Los Angeles, California, CA 90039, USA

TO VISIT BEFORE YOU DIE BECAUSE

The only Neutra house regularly open to the public is a nimble experiment in urban living.

When Richard Neutra (1892-1970) received an interest-free loan from Dutch industrial and architecture fan Cees Hendrik van der Leeuw in 1931, he decided to use it to build his own family home. He found a beautiful plot at Silver Lake in California and designed a radically modern house that is both airy and geometrically constructed. Neutra lived there from 1932 with his wife Dione and their three children. Unfortunately, the original Neutra VDL House burned down in 1963. In the inferno, the library and all of Neutra's plans and notes were lost. Instead of mourning, the architect simply rebuilt it, together with his son Dion. Anyone looking through the adjustments can easily estimate how revolutionary the design must have been in the interbellum period. In 1980, Neutra's widow donated the home to California State Polytechnic University, whose students from the College of Environmental Design still give Saturday tours. The house has been undergoing an intensive restoration programme since 2008, although there is also room for artist residencies.

www.neutra-vdl.org

The Americas     USA

# 45   PALMER HOUSE (1952)

By Frank Lloyd Wright
227 Orchard Hills Drive, Ann Arbor, Michigan, MI 48104, USA

TO VISIT
BEFORE YOU DIE
BECAUSE

This house offers a glimpse of the tranquil life, all through the prism of a triangle.

William Palmer, a professor specialising in economics, and his wife Mary together harboured dreams of a tranquil life. They set up residence in the heart of nature, at the end of an unpaved road, about a kilometre from the University of Michigan. Frank Lloyd Wright (1867 - 1959) designed an incredible set of plans and also oversaw the construction of their home. The design module for the house was the equilateral triangle and that is the most obvious and predominant design element, even for much of the built-in furniture. The house is covered by a spectacular wide-span roof that overhangs each of the three wings. It embodies the Usonian models, a concept invented by Wright that marks the birth of an architecture specifically based on the American way of life and integrated into the natural landscape of the United States. Usonia is an adaptation of the acronym 'Usona', which denotes 'United States of North America'. The Palmer house is available for overnight rental.

www.flwpalmerhouse.com

The Americas  USA

## 46 THE SHEATS-GOLDSTEIN HOUSE (1961–1963)

By John Lautner
Angelo View Drive, Beverly Hills, California, CA 90210, USA

**TO VISIT BEFORE YOU DIE BECAUSE**

This futuristic eagle's nest has appeared in cult movies, including *The Big Lebowski* and *Charlie's Angels*.

John Lautner (1911–1994) trained under Frank Lloyd Wright at Taliesin and was one of the most talented figures to emerge from Wright's school of architecture. What makes him stand out is a spectacular form of architecture that is at once organic and futuristic. Perched high in Beverly Hills, the house was originally built for Helen and Paul Sheats, an artist and a university professor respectively. The plan is bold, with no right angles, instead presenting a futuristic geometry based on the triangle that was so dear to Lautner's heart. The businessman James Goldstein bought the house in 1972 and, together with Lautner, he completely renovated it over the course of more than twenty years. Numerous modifications were made, including an Infinity Edge tennis court and a nightclub. The cheaper original materials were replaced, and John Lautner designed new furniture, such as the huge cantilevered sofas in the living room. Below the residence is James Turrell's skyspace facility, also known as Above Horizon. This incredible setting has inspired many films, including *The Big Lebowski*. Goldstein donated the house to the Los Angeles County Museum of Art in 2016.
John Lautner before his passing remodeled the original structure and created a master-plan withadditional structures and uses on the expanded property. Lautner's project architect Duncan Nicholson took over the project with his partner James Perry. Work continues on a major entertainment and sports facility, the 'Club James', inspired by Lautner. Tours are available by appointment only.

The Americas — USA

## 47 PRAIRIE HOUSE (1961)

By Herb Greene
550 48th Avenue Northeast, Norman, Oklahoma, OK 73026, USA

**TO VISIT BEFORE YOU DIE BECAUSE**

This house is an organic shelter, made to live in.

The Prairie House is an icon of organic modernism, a modern architectural movement which strives for a perfect harmony between nature and architecture. Admittedly, architect Herb Greene (1929) may not be as famous as his teachers Frank Lloyd Wright and Bruce Goff, but his work is highly authentic - particularly this Prairie House, which he built for himself on the prairies of Oklahoma in 1961. Although atypical in shape, the private dwelling is perfectly at home in the vast windblown landscape. Unfinished cedar shingles on the outside and inside give the home the appearance of a ramshackle dwelling. This conveys the sense of a structure that looks and feels like a shelter, offering comfort and safety. At the same time, the organic shape also has something vernacular, the appearance of an improvised cabin rather than an architect's design. When the house was completed, it was immediately picked up by the architectural press of the day. And even today people never tire of hearing about Herb Greene's eccentric creation. Until recently you could stay in the Prairie House, but it is currently being restored. The owner is likely to reopen this unique home to the public when the structure has been fully renovated.

No official website

The Americas  USA

# 48 SCHINDLER HOUSE (1922)

By Rudolph Schindler
833 North Kings Road, West Hollywood, Los Angeles, California, CA 90069, USA

**TO VISIT BEFORE YOU DIE BECAUSE**

Observe the first real Modernist house in America, a true departure from existing residential architecture.

Rudolph Schindler (1887-1953) and Richard Neutra, who studied together in Vienna, were among the first generation of modern architects who moved from Europe to the States. Initially, both worked in Chicago, the city of Frank Lloyd Wright, where Schindler was able to join Wright's famous studio in Oak Park, working there until 1921. Immediately after, Schindler began his own practice, and set about designing his own home. It was a house that he and his wife Pauline would share with friends, the engineer Clyde Chace and his wife Marian. This experiment in communal living called for an unorthodox layout that provided shared living areas and private space. In fact, the house consists of four separate studios around a central room with a hearth, a shared kitchen, and a private patio for each couple. To ensure flexible circulation, rather than fitting the studios with standard doors, he used sliding walls. With his unadorned design in glass, concrete, wood, and linen, Schindler casually fashioned a blueprint for a new, modern style of (communal) living in California.

www.makcenter.org/sites/schindler-house

## 49 SAARINEN HOUSE (1930)

By Eliel Saarinen
39221 Woodward Ave Box 801, Cranbrook, Bloomfield Hills, Michigan, MI 48304, USA

**TO VISIT BEFORE YOU DIE BECAUSE**

The home of the Saarinen family showcases their elegant design talent.

In the world of design and architecture, the name Saarinen is world famous. Perhaps the best known is Eero Saarinen (1910-1961): the Finnish American designer of the TWA Flight Center at JFK Airport (now a hotel) and the Tulip Chair for Knoll. His father Eliel (1873-1950) was already a celebrity in his native country, feted as the most important figure in the Finnish Jugendstil movement when, in 1923, he emigrated to the States. There, he expanded his career as an architect and as a professor at the Cranbrook Academy of Art, the American Bauhaus, where designers Florence Knoll, Harry Bertoia, and Charles and Ray Eames trained. Saarinen senior designed two school buildings, a museum and his own private residence on Cranbrook campus. In terms of architecture and interior, that 1930 house tells the Saarinen family saga: the U-shaped house is a delicate blend of Arts and Crafts influences and Art Deco, with interior textiles by his wife Loja and early furniture designs by son Eero. Now open to the public, the house is part of the Cranbrook Art Museum site.

The Americas — USA

# 50 WICHITA / DYMAXION HOUSE (1929–1947)

By Richard Buckminster Fuller
The Henry Ford Museum, 20900 Oakwood Boulevard, Dearborn, Michigan, MI 48124, USA

**TO VISIT BEFORE YOU DIE BECAUSE**

Circular and lightweight, Buckminster Fuller's modular home was ahead of its time.

The modular prefab house is a recurring fetish for many generations of architects and designers; just think of Jean Prouvé, Richard Buckminster Fuller, and Matti Suuronen. Prouvé developed different types of quickly buildable emergency houses in wood and steel, Suuronen devised a UFO-shaped plastic living unit that could 'land' on any terrain. But the most visionary housing prophet of the 20th century was undoubtedly Richard Buckminster Fuller (1895-1983). He was obsessed with lightweight architecture that could be fabricated on a large scale and used as little energy and material as possible. At the end of the 1920s the engineer was already making a furore with his 'Dymaxion' project, shortly before 'Dynamic Maximum Tension'. Even after World War II, Buckminster Fuller continued to work on a prototype for a lightweight house in steel and aluminium, inspired by technology from the aviation and automobile industries. Despite the ingenious design – a circular house wrapped around a functional core and supported by a single mast – and the orders that rolled in, few homes were actually built. One of the rare prototypes, called 'Wichita House,' is now in the Henry Ford Museum in Michigan.

The Americas — USA

# 51 TYLER RESIDENCE (1953)

By John Lautner
3612 Woodhill Canyon Road, Studio City, California, CA 91604, USA

**TO VISIT BEFORE YOU DIE BECAUSE**

Perhaps the pinnacle for the use of the triangle in architecture, this Studio City property is an iconic Modernist home.

Nestled among the trees of Studio City, the Tyler Residence is a type of cabin where wood predominates both outside and inside the house. This is Lautner (1911 - 1994) once again, creating a total work of art that shows respect for its environment and a penchant for the repetition of forms. As so often elsewhere, he uses the shape of the triangle in all sorts of different ways, from the skylight to the shower, in the shape of the steps, and even for the peak of the roof. The residence was used as the location for the film *The Human Contract* (2008).

No official website

The Americas    USA

# 52 STAHL HOUSE / CASE STUDY HOUSE #22 (1960)

By Pierre Koenig
1635 Woods Drive, West Hollywood, Los Angeles, California, CA 90069, USA

**TO VISIT BEFORE YOU DIE BECAUSE**

In the most iconic of the Case Study Houses, relish this creation's panoramic view of Los Angeles.

As part of the Case Study Program, architects such as Pierre Koenig, Richard Neutra, Charles and Ray Eames, and Craig Ellwood were asked to design replicable affordable homes, 'with an emphasis on new materials or new building techniques'. Of the 36 homes and apartments, 20 have been preserved homes and apartments have been preserved for posterity. Most are privately owned, except for the Stahl House and the Eames House, which offer pre-booked guided tours. Pierre Koenig (1925-2004) designed his own low-budget home with a steel frame as a student in 1950. The Case Study Program gave him the opportunity to realise two houses with a similar steel frame: Bailey House (Case Study House # 21, 1958) and Stahl House (Case Study House #22, 1960). The latter has acquired cult status for the panoramic view of Los Angeles from the swimming pool and living space, which overlooks the hill. The house is spatially organised around the pool in an L-shape. Structurally, however, the Stahl House is very simple: using commercially available materials, Koenig created a transparent residence of steel girders and sheet glass.

www.stahlhouse.com

## 53 TALIESIN EAST & WEST (1911–1959)

By Frank Lloyd Wright – 5607 County Rd C, Spring Green, Wisconsin, WI 53588 (Taliesin East) / 12621 N Frank Lloyd Wright Blvd, Scottsdale, AZ 85259, USA (Taliesin West)

TO VISIT BEFORE YOU DIE BECAUSE

These buildings represent the autobiography of the master of 20th-century architecture.

Taliesin East is the summer residence that Frank Lloyd Wright (1867 - 1959) started to build in 1911, following divorce from his first wife. It was the scene of a terrible tragedy and multiple fires, which meant that it had already been rebuilt on three occasions by 1959. The site sits on the hill that had been Wright's favourite since childhood, in the valley of the Wisconsin River that was inhabited by his Welsh grandparents. The term 'Taliesin' comes from the name of a Welsh druid. It was here that Wright conceived many of his most famous buildings, including Fallingwater. In 1932 he and his third wife Olga established the Taliesin Fellowship, a community of apprentices who lived and worked at Taliesin, an estate that included some 250 hectares of workable land, as well as Wright's studio, music rooms, lodgings, and archives. The aim of each apprenticeship was 'to develop a well correlated, creative human being with a wide horizon but capable of effective concentration of his faculties upon the circumstance in which he lives.' Richard Schindler and Richard Neutra were just two of the architects who took part in this training scheme.

Taliesin West is nestled into the desert foothills of the McDowell Mountains in Arizona. It was Wright's beloved winter home and the bustling headquarters of the Taliesin Fellowship. Deeply connected to the desert from which it was forged, Taliesin West has an almost prehistoric grandeur. Today it is home to the Frank Lloyd Wright Foundation and the Taliesin School of Architecture. Both complexes are listed as UNESCO World Heritage Sites.

The Americas · USA

## 54 UMBRELLA HOUSE (1953)

By Paul Rudolph
1300 Westway Drive, Sarasota, Florida, FL 34236, USA

TO VISIT BEFORE YOU DIE BECAUSE

See inside a house hidden by the most stunning umbrella in architectural history.

Like I.M. Pei, Paul Rudolph (1918 - 1997) was one of Walter Gropius' most famous students at Harvard. Although not Rudolph's most iconic residence, Umbrella House (1953) certainly lives up to its name. A monumental awning that mimics a U-shaped umbrella shades the entire house from the merciless sun in Sarasota, Florida. The original tent-like 'sun canopy' that floated above the house was a wood structure, but was irreparably damaged by a tropical storm in the 1960s. It was not until 2015 that the house received a new 'umbrella', for which it was immediately granted the award of excellence for Historic Preservation and Rehabilitation. It was the energetic property developer Philip Hiss who commissioned Rudolph in 1953 for 'an iconic home'. The architect, then living and working in Florida, built several landmark public buildings in the area, cementing Sarasota's reputation as a destination for devotees of mid-century modernist architecture. The Sarasota Architectural Foundation regularly organises tours of the Umbrella House.

www.saf-srq.org/architecture/umbrella-house

The Americas — Venezuela

# 55 VILLA PLANCHART (1953–1957)

By Gio Ponti
Calle La Colina, Caracas Metropolitan District 1060, Miranda, Venezuela

**TO VISIT BEFORE YOU DIE BECAUSE**

A giant abstract sculpture with a view of the mountains, this house transposes an Italian dream to the tropics of Venezuela.

'Your house will be like a great butterfly perched on a hill', wrote Gio Ponti (1891–1979) in a letter to Armando and Anala Planchart, lovers and collectors of modern architecture who would be the future owners of the house. Located on the heights of Caracas, the Villa Planchart is the transposition of an Italian dream to the tropical flora and foliage of Venezuela. The façades form screens suspended from the roof, whose contours are underlined by a lighting system at night. Inside there is a genuine spectacle of colour from room to room. It is a multicoloured kaleidoscope from floor to ceiling, with all sorts of features, including marble mosaics, yellow-striped ceilings, and woodwork adorned with painted geometric patterns. All of the materials were shipped from Italy, from the pieces of marble to the different types of wood, as well as all the furniture and objects.

Ponti designed many of the features in this house, such as the fitted windows that allow art objects to be displayed, the pivoting shelves, and the integrated planters to hold the orchids that Armando cultivated in his greenhouse.

www.villaplanchart.blogspot.com

Asia — India

## 56 JEANNERET HOUSE (1954)

By Pierre Jeanneret
57, Uttar Marg, Sukhna Lake, Sector 5, Chandigarh 160005, India

**TO VISIT BEFORE YOU DIE BECAUSE**

Understanding this house gives visitors an insight into the architectural vision behind the new city of Chandigarh.

In 1951, Le Corbusier and his cousin Pierre Jeanneret were commissioned by Jawaharlal Nehru, the Indian Prime Minister, to build the city of the future in Chandigarh, the first new city in a newly independent India. Pierre Jeanneret (1896 - 1967) was deeply marked by this enormous project and settled for a period of 11 years in this house that has now been transformed into a museum in his honour. Charged with furnishing the city's institutional buildings, he called on local craftsmen and used regional materials better suited to the climate to create iconic furniture that would leave its mark on 20th-century design. His house makes use of river pebbles and red clay, which contrast with the white-coated surfaces. The brick-lattice masonry, raw concrete surfaces, and narrow openings to trap the light mark the architectural identity of Chandigarh. Make sure to visit the entire city, which is absolutely remarkable.

www.museumsofindia.org/museum/530/pierre-jeanneret-museum

Asia — Israel

# 57 WEIZMANN HOUSE (1937)

By Erich Mendelsohn
Herzl 234, Rehovot, Israel

TO VISIT BEFORE YOU DIE BECAUSE

This house, because of its site, climate, and landscape, and its organisation around a cylindrical stairwell, offers the perfect opportunity to discover Israeli architecture.

Produced for Chaim Weizmann, the first president of the state of Israel, and his wife Vera Weizmann, this is the first building constructed in Israel by the German architect Eric Mendelsohn (1887–1953). Mendelsohn's designs of the 1930s had a big influence on the local architecture of Jerusalem and Tel Aviv. Architects in Israel at the time were very much absorbed by the Bauhaus, which idealised a future of modernity and creativity. Located at the top of a hill, the house offers a breathtaking view of the coastal plain. Its architectural design expresses the synthesis between European Modernism and traditional Mediterranean influences. The house is organised around a central tower which houses an extremely elegant spiral staircase. At the foot of the house, a mirrored swimming pool gives a reflection of the house. Today, the Weizmann House is part of the Weizmann Scientific Institute.

www.chaimweizmann.org.il/

Asia — Sri Lanka

# 58 BAWA HOUSE (1960–1970)

By Geoffrey Bawa
Number 11, 33rd Lane, Bagatelle Road, Colombo 03, Sri Lanka

TO VISIT BEFORE YOU DIE BECAUSE

Admire the work of Sri Lanka's premier architect in this house, an essay in architectural bricolage.

Geoffrey Bawa (1919–2003) is the César Manrique of Sri Lanka: a modern architect who created the identity of an island. His incredible achievements throughout South Asia shouldn't go unsung. Bawa himself shuttled between his house in Colombo and Lunuganga, his paradise country retreat on Dedduwa Lake. Both are now hotels, which you can also visit as a non-guest. Bawa's private Colombo home is a wonderful example of his organic architecture. With patios, loggias, and interior courtyards, he conjures a fluid boundary between architecture and nature, even in the heart of a bustling city. His own house in Colombo is actually quite complex, purely because – just like Haus Ungers in Cologne (p.183) – it has evolved spontaneously over the years. Within the space of ten years, Bawa was able to purchase four different adjoining bungalows, which he gradually transformed into one large estate.

'Architectural bricolage' may sound pejorative, but for Bawa that strategy was essential: both houses are spontaneous laboratories for his ideas regarding architecture and landscape. His Colombo home is still an oasis in the city, where a number of his private properties await discovery. And best of all: you can spend the night there.

www.geoffreybawa.com/number-11

Asia — Sri Lanka

# 59 LUNUGANGA (1948–1997)

By Geoffrey Bawa
Dedduwa, Bentota, Sri Lanka

**TO VISIT BEFORE YOU DIE BECAUSE**

Overnight in Geoffrey Bawa's countr home and gardens, his experimental laboratory for new ideas.

Geoffrey Bawa (1919–2003) initially studied law at Cambridge, but when he arrived in Sri Lanka, the illegitimate son of an English gentleman, he bought an abandoned rubber plantation in 1948. He started its renovation as a self-taught artist, but during the process he decided to study architecture in London. Lunuganga would eventually become the masterpiece of his so-called 'tropical modernism', characterised as a blend of Eastern, Western, Classical, Modernist and 'vernacular' architecture: buildings that arose spontaneously, without an architect. The main house always remained the core of his paradise, but he added a design studio and guest house, among other things. Between the 1950s and 1990s he continued to embellish the estate, until the house and the surrounding gardens achieved a perfect symbiosis. Just like Lina Bo Bardi in her Casa de Vidro (1951) (p.27), Bawa formulated the ideal answer here to the history of the site, the tropical climate, and the vegetation of the island. His design is so intuitive that it invites you to believe that this is how the site has always been. Lunuganga is now run as a boutique hotel, but you can buy a ticket to visit the estate and the fantastic gardens.

www.geoffreybawa.com/lunuganga

Europe — Austria

# 60 DOMENIG STEINHAUS (1980)

By Günther Domenig
Uferweg 31, 9552 Steindorf am Ossiacher See, Austria

TO VISIT BEFORE YOU DIE BECAUSE

See regional landscape elements transformed into fascinating architecture with a noticeable spatial intensity.

Although Günther Domenig (1934-2012) was one of Austria's leading post-war architects, he had to move heaven and earth to realise his home in Steindorf. His neighbours flatly rejected his plans and, in the end, construction dragged on for over 20 years. The unique home of this avant-garde architect stands on the edge of Lake Ossiach, a large lake in the Austrian state of Carinthia. Domenig conceived his house as a kind of geological primal force: a quasi-crystalline composition of polygonal volumes that, like tectonic plates, are mapped with fault lines. The whimsical assembly of free volumes is reminiscent of the work of Frank Gehry, Daniel Libeskind, and early designs of Zaha Hadid. Domenig translated the mountainous environment into a living deconstructivist sculpture, which, although experimental, does not feel alien to its environment. Although many assert that this 'stone house' is his masterpiece, the architect is best known for his large-scale public commissions and participations in the Venice Biennale.

architektur-kaernten.at/medien/
domenig-steinhaus-spektakulaere-architektur-erleben

Europe  Austria

# 61 VILLA BEER (1929–1930)

By Josef Frank and Oscar Wlach
Wenzgasse 12, 1130 Wien, Austria

TO VISIT BEFORE YOU DIE BECAUSE

**This Modernist and humanist 'cruiseliner' helps you understand the relationship between space and state of mind.**

Built in the aristocratic suburbs of Vienna for the rubber-sole manufacturer Julius Beer and his wife, this building is considered to be the manifesto of Josef Frank (1885–1967), an architect greatly influenced by influenced by Adolf Loos' Villa Müller in Prague. Frank is regarded as one of the founders of Swedish modern design, and in contrast to the rigidity for which his international colleagues in the Modern movement are often reproached, he liked to work on the psychological effects of the layout of the living space and especially its furniture. He believed that people should enjoy a different spatial experience in each of the different zones of the house, and thus be able to find a room to suit any particular mood. He is also known for his magnificent wallpaper and textile designs with multicoloured plant motifs. He practised a form of "Human Modernism" that was misunderstood in Vienna, eventually leading him to settle in Sweden in 1934, where his career was fully recognised.

www.azw.at/en/event/guided-tours-of-villa-beer/

Europe    Belgium

# 62 HÔTEL MAX HALLET (1903–1906)

By Victor Horta
346 Avenue Louise, 1050 Brussels, Belgium

TO VISIT
BEFORE YOU DIE
BECAUSE

This gem is inhabited by a collector of Horta houses.

Built by Victor Horta (1861 - 1947) for the lawyer and politician Max Hallet, the Hôtel Max Hallet symbolises a late flourish for the Art Nouveau style. The discreet luxury of its sober façade houses a refined interior made up of curves, counter-curves, and lavish materials. The central stairwell looks like a bouquet of flowers. Its mural frescoes are painted with hundreds of roses – the choice of the lady of the house. Monumental in size, it leads to an elegant three-lobed glazed conservatory, which serves as a winter garden. The walls of the living room and the dining room are covered with fine silk tapestries that have floral motifs. Very much a space for reception, the venue also features a musicians' gallery on the second floor. Now lived in, it has been meticulously restored to its original glory by its owner, a lover of Victor Horta's work.

www.victorhorta.be

Europe  Belgium

# 63 HORTA MUSEUM (1898–1901)

By Victor Horta
25 Rue Américaine, 1060 Brussels, Belgium

TO VISIT BEFORE YOU DIE BECAUSE

Behold a breathtaking 'total work of art' by the master of the Art Nouveau style.

Victor Horta's home and office are a veritable calling card of the talents and uniqueness of this master of the Art Nouveau style. Horta (1861 - 1947) was the first architect to bring steel into the heart of private homes, a material which had until then been reserved for use in railway stations, greenhouses, and industrial buildings.

Horta once famously said of his organic Art Nouveau practices: 'it is not the flower that I like to take as the decorative element, but the stem'. This dynamic quotation seems to be a font of inspiration in his constructions. With Horta, there is nothing random about the way things are built and the form is always suited to the function. Wherever movement is required (on the stairs, or in the spaces of circulation), the lines are undulating and there is motion in the forms. By contrast, the areas dedicated to rest (the living room and dining room) are symmetrical, with calming lines. Nature is omnipresent in the house: the walls are painted with frescoes which incorporate organic motifs produced in graduated shades moving up towards the skylight, itself filtered through a canopy of coloured glass.

www.hortamuseum.be

Europe — Belgium

# 64 HÔTEL SOLVAY (1895–1903)

By Victor Horta
224 Avenue Louise, 1050 Brussels, Belgium

**TO VISIT BEFORE YOU DIE BECAUSE**

This Art Nouveau town house, showcasing precious materials and expensive details, is a timeless box of architectural jewels.

Built for Armand Solvay – the son of the Belgian industrialist Ernest Solvay – the Hotel Solvay is one of Victor Horta's (1861 - 1947) most innovative buildings, one for which he was given an unlimited budget and carte blanche to complete. A venue for parties and receptions, it features a remarkable double-flighted staircase covered by a skylight made in multicoloured Tiffany glass. The transition from one material to another – incorporating wood, bronze, marble, and stone – is handled so subtly that it is barely noticeable. The staircase leads to the upper ground floor where the living room and dining room are located, enclosed by glass walls that can be opened to form a single space that then covers pretty much the entire house. The innovation of the plan is avant-garde. Horta draws axes that invite the inhabitants to circulate within the house via an 'architectural promenade', much like what Le Corbusier would go on to favour. A genuine work of art, the Hotel Solvay features its original furniture, carpets, marble, stained glass, paintings, and lighting.

Europe  Belgium

# 65 HÔTEL OTLET (1894–1898)

By Octave van Rysselberghe and Henry van de Velde
13 Rue de Florence, 1000 Brussels, Belgium

TO VISIT BEFORE YOU DIE BECAUSE

Bask in this house's elegance and see the stairway to an Art Nouveau heaven.

Built for the lawyer Paul Otlet (1868–1944), this house is one of the pioneering works of Art Nouveau in Belgium. From the façade alone, it is possible to read the plan of the house and even guess at the way of life of its inhabitants. The ground floor is devoted to daily life, containing the dining room, kitchen, and living rooms. Upstairs is the domain of intellectual activities, with its library, music room, study, and spaces reserved for the private collection. The whole is connected by an impressive central spiral staircase that leads to each of the different areas – a perfectly integrated work of art by Henry van de Velde. Interior windows glazed with coloured stained glass and a loggia maximise light and are typical of Art Nouveau. The juxtaposition between the respective activities of the day and night is reflected in the contrasting treatment of the façade: the dining room is open at the corner of the two façades, while the bedroom on the first floor is blind. Both traditional and modern, the façade presents a particularly successful play of solids and voids.

Europe — Belgium

# 66 VILLA EMPAIN (1931–1934)

By Michel Polak
67 Avenue Franklin Roosevelt, 1050 Brussels, Belgium

TO VISIT BEFORE YOU DIE BECAUSE

A part of Brussels' architectural heritage, this mansion, with its modern swimming pool, is a hidden Art Deco gem in the city.

Louis Empain, the son of the businessman Baron Edouard Empain, commissioned the design of his house from Michel Polak (1885–1948). At only 22 years of age, the young Louis was already interested in the architecture of his time, with a passion for Art Deco and the experimental approaches of the Bauhaus. These two trends are certainly evident in this house: we find the luxury of the materials dear to Art Deco (the polished granite of the façade; the gold, marble, and precious woods); and the pure, simple lines of modernist architecture. The swimming pool that extends beyond the villa is one of the most modern of the period and is still much admired. Rumour has it that Louis Empain never actually moved in, but it is likely that he lived here for at least a year. Following a mystical revelation, he vowed to devote his life to others and donated his villa to the Belgian state in 1937. Magnificently restored, it is now home to the Boghossian Foundation, a centre for art and dialogue between the cultures of East and West.

www.villaempain.com

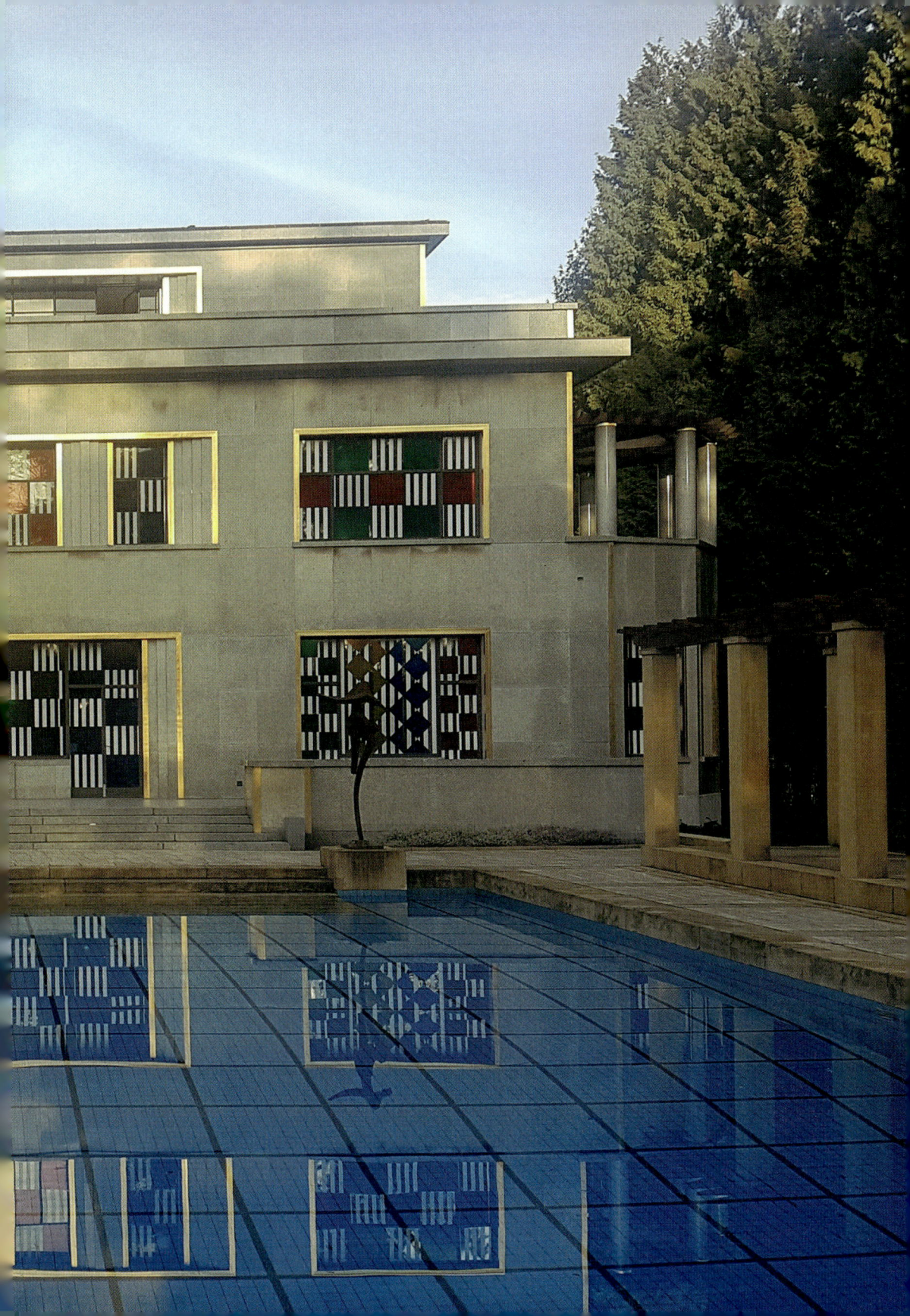

Europe — Belgium

# 67 MAISON BERTEAUX (1936)

By Louis Herman de Koninck
59 Avenue du Fort-Jaco, 1180 Uccle, Belgium

TO VISIT BEFORE YOU DIE BECAUSE

Complete with shimmering façades, this house is an outstanding example of stripped-down, contemporary architecture.

A leading figure of Belgian Modernism, Louis Herman de Koninck (1896–1984) built this house for the engineer Raoul Berteaux and his wife, who was one of the first female surgeons. At a time when the world was discovering new technologies, and attitudes were radically changing, ocean liners proved to be an inexhaustible source of inspiration for architects, who used portholes, tubular railings, and rounded angles in their designs. The façades are sails of moulded concrete, a technique invented by de Koninck that consists of pouring concrete into wooden forms, thereby giving the impression that the house is built in one piece. The façades shimmer in the light because the sails are covered with Cimorné – a contraction of 'ciment-orné' – a layer of cement that has marble and crushed glass sprayed onto it while it is still fresh. In the kitchen is a reissue of the first Belgian fitted kitchen, the CUBEX, invented by de Koninck himself at the end of the 1920s.

www.arkadia.be

Europe — Belgium

# 68 DE BEIR HOUSE / 'BLACK HOUSE' (1924)

By Huib Hoste
Belgium – Dumortierlaan 8, 8300 Knokke, Belgium

TO VISIT BEFORE YOU DIE BECAUSE

This is the best example of De Stijl in Belgium.

The Black House in Knokke is the most unique Modernist building on the Belgian coast. In 2001, it was preserved as a listed building in the nick of time. Huib Hoste (1881 - 1957) designed the house in 1924 for Raymond de Beir, a doctor with many connections in the art world. Consultation rooms occupied the ground floor, and the doctor and his family lived upstairs. The separate functions are translated visually in the façade: the plinth is in Boom tiles and the upper storeys are clad in black cement. Although extended and restored on several occasions during the 20th century, there is no mistaking the radicality of the building's original design. Hoste was clearly inspired by the geometric modernism of De Stijl, with the floors, window frames, doors, and stained-glass windows rendered in primary colours à la Van Doesburg and Mondrian. The interior was styled in collaboration with artist Victor Servranckx. When Dr de Beir lived there, his 'Black House' was a meeting place for the artistic avant-garde of the day. And thanks to the current owner, it continues to be a home for art. The owner recently started leasing the residence to galleries, which host an exhibition programme starting in the spring. A perfect opportunity to peek inside this landmark building.

no official website

Europe — Belgium

# 69 RENAAT BRAEM HUIS (1958)

By Renaat Braem
23 Menegemlei, 2100 Antwerp, Belgium

TO VISIT BEFORE YOU DIE BECAUSE

Enjoy this house's functional use of colour and bold design furniture, all created in Antwerp by a man who thought Belgium was the ugliest country in the world.

Renaat Braem's private residence is one of the most fascinating in post-war Belgian architecture. Initially, architect Braem (1910-2001) had plans to turn the working home into an organic sculpture in brick and concrete - like his pavilion in Middelheim Park - but it proved to be too expensive. So he reduced his design to a composition of stacked blocks, with a concrete and brick skeleton. He described his home as: 'A composition of space and time on a human scale. A poetic musical composition in which different rhythms are entwined, where you can feel at one with nature.' In keeping with the philosophy of his teacher Le Corbusier, Braem devised a colour scheme that amplified both the sense of space and the atmosphere. Sixty years later, Braem's home remains one of his most personal and radical designs. He lived there from 1958 to 1997, but in 1999 he decided to donate his house and its entire contents to the Flemish state. The house underwent thorough restoration in 2003 and became the second architectural house museum in Belgium, after the Horta Museum in Brussels.

Europe                    Czech Republic

# 70 BRUMMEL HOUSE (1928–1929)

By Adolf Loos
Husova 58, 301 00 Plzeň 3, Czech Republic

**TO VISIT BEFORE YOU DIE BECAUSE**

This seemingly unspectacular restored villa is the best preserved and most representative of Loos' important early-modern architecture in Plzeň.

Outwardly cold and austere, the façade of this house hides a true multicoloured architectural gem. It was designed by Adolf Loos (1870 - 1933) for Jan Brummel, his wife Jana, and her mother, Hedvika Liebstein. On the first floor of the house there is a separate apartment for each generation, perfectly designed so that everyone could live independently, but with a common dining room so they could still come together. The house and its inhabitants share a dramatic history. After the Nazi occupation of Czechoslovakia in 1939, the Brummel family was deported to concentration camps. Hedvika died, while Jan and Jana survived. At the end of the 1970s, the house was saved from demolition and returned after the Velvet Revolution in the 1990s to the family. They restored it in 2001, which continued untill 2015, the year it was opened to the public. By some miracle, the interior fittings of the apartment have been preserved, including the built-in furniture designed by the architect. Close by, you can also visit another of Loos' creations, the Kraus Apartment, which boasts an amazing dining room bedecked with green marble-tiled walls and mirrors.

www.adolfloospilsen.cz

Europe — Czech Republic

# 71 VILLA WINTERNITZ (1932)

By Adolf Loos
Na Cihlářce 10, Prague 5, Czech Republic

**TO VISIT BEFORE YOU DIE BECAUSE**

The last private residence completed by Adolf Loos, Villa Winternitz boasts built-in furniture, beautiful materials, and unexpected colours.

Anyone with even a passing interest in architecture knows about the Prague house, Villa Müller (1930), designed by Adolf Loos (1870 - 1933). But few are aware that Loos built a villa for Josef Winternitz, lawyer to businessman Frantisek Müller. In 1931 and 1932, the architects were commissioned to design a home for Josef, his wife Jenny, daughter Suzana, and son Peter. The differences between the two are numerous: Loos used far less lavish materials for Villa Winternitz and his 'Raumplan' was much simpler. Yet Loos' signature is still in evidence. Villa Winternitz was the last house he finished: shortly afterwards the Austrian architect died in a sanatorium in Kalksburg. The Winternitz family lived there until 1941, when the Nazis confiscated it and sent the family to Auschwitz. Josef and Peter died there, Jenny and Suzana miraculously survived. After the war, they were unable to reclaim the villa because they could not afford the inheritance tax. In the end, it was purchased by the city of Prague, and turned into a nursery school and artist's home. Thanks to the efforts of Josef's grandson, it has now been completely restored and opened to the public.

www.loosovavila.cz

Europe  Czech Republic

## 72 THE HIRSCH APARTMENT (1927–1929)

By Adolf Loos
U Starého hřbitova 40/6, 110 00 Prague 1 - Josefov, Czech Republic

**TO VISIT BEFORE YOU DIE BECAUSE**

This apartment contains one of the most complete collections of original Adolf Loos' furniture in the world.

Adolf Loos (1870–1933) did not belong to a clearly defined architectural movement. An ardent defender of simplicity, he considered ornament an artifice. His interiors are simple, and the luxury lies in the choice of materials, such as mirrors, marble, and mahogany. Loos created several masterpieces in Bohemia that fully testified to his refined design. In 1907 in Pilsen, he designed the house of the entrepreneurial couple Martha and Wilhelm Hirsch. It was not discovered until the 1980s that this was not in fact his only creation for the Hirsch family. In 1927 he also designed an apartment for Wilhelm's son Richard. This apartment was in the same building as the better-known Hirsch apartment, but was located on a different floor, rediscovered only in 1988. The apartment was preserved and moved to Prague, to an apartment of the same configuration near the Jewish cemetery. It serves today as an art gallery and auction house.

## 73 VILLA MÜLLER (1929–1930)

By Adolf Loos
Nad Hradním vodojem 14/162, Prague 6, Czech Republic

**TO VISIT BEFORE YOU DIE BECAUSE**

This austere cube-shaped villa manifests all of its richness in its interior, with a dramatic staging of different height levels for various rooms based on their function and symbolic importance.

This villa was built for Milada and František Müller. František co-owned the large construction company Müller & Kapsa, which played an important role in construction in Czechoslovakia between the wars. František acquired a plot of land near the castle in Prague, with a grandiose view of the city centre providing plenty of inspiration for the architect. From the outside, the villa is a simple cube, its surprisingly austere façades punctuated by the narrow yellow windows that are characteristic of Loos' work. For him, a house should not be built for the benefit of passers-by, but for its inhabitants. Inside, Adolf Loos (1870 - 1933) implements his concept of 'Raumplan', a three-dimensional plan with rooms of varying heights, depending on their importance. He gives particular attention to distinguishing between day zones and night zones, and public and private spaces, which he links together by means of staircases. The spaces combine to form a surprising sense of harmony between the functional austerity of the service areas and the more classical English style of the reception areas. Most of the original furniture and works of art are still preserved.

Europe — Denmark

## 74 FINN JUHL'S HUS (1942)

By Finn Juhl
Kratvænget 15 in Ordrup, 2920 Charlottenlund, Denmark

TO VISIT BEFORE YOU DIE BECAUSE

**A textbook example of Scandinavian design, this house blends art with architecture, colour with calm, and building with nature.**

Finn Juhl's own house – built for himself and his first wife – is a paragon of Danish modern design and architecture. The residence is a simple L-shaped open-plan bungalow in Charlottenlund, on the outskirts of Copenhagen. Despite Juhl's bold use of colour, the house exudes serenity. The restored interior boasts Juhl's (1912–1989) original furniture designs, juxtaposed with numerous works of art by Danish artists such as Vilhelm Lundstrøm, Egill Jacobsen, Asger Jorn, and Richard Mortensen. Given that Juhl originally planned to train as an art historian, it is not surprising that art was a key feature of the interior. 'Art has always been my main source of inspiration,' he said. 'I am fascinated by shapes that have gravity and create visual lightness.' One of the first things that hits you when you enter the house is the fact that Juhl designed it from the inside out, utilising materials and colours in perfect balance with the surrounding nature. While he was designing his home, Juhl was still working at Vilhelm Lauritzen's office and had designed several pieces of furniture for Niels Vodder. Juhl's House has been open to the public since 2008.

Europe · Finland

## 75 AALTO HOUSE (1935–1936)

By Alvar Aalto
Riihitie 20, Munkkiniemi, 00330 Helsinki, Finland

**TO VISIT BEFORE YOU DIE BECAUSE**

View the 'chicken coop' which best captures Alvar and Aino Aalto's creative partnership.

'What kind of weird chicken coop are they building here?' Even while under construction, Alvar and Aino Aalto's private home attracted mixed comments. The design is unusual, with a windowless, plain façade facing onto the street. But anyone wanting to visit Aalto's 'chicken coop' today can only do so by joining a pre-booked guided tour. The private home has become a museum dedicated to the Aaltos' dynamic, creative partnership. Alvar and Aino lived there from 1936 until their deaths in 1976 and 1949 respectively. Alvar's indoor design studio was in use until 1955, the year he built a new studio just down the street. Their home remains Aalto's most intimate realisation, conceived as an ode to the potency of natural materials such as wood, natural stone, and brick. For the Aaltos, their private home was primarily a kind of laboratory; yet the design is a work of art, with bespoke furniture and fittings. The original furnishings have been preserved. The piano belonged to Aino, and the lamp that stands on it was a gift to Alvar from his fellow designer Poul Henningsen.

www.alvaraalto.fi/en/location/the-aalto-house

Europe — Finland

## 76 FUTURO HOUSE (1968)

By Matti Suuronen
WeeGee Expo Center, Ahertajantie 5, 02100 Espoo, Finland
(and various sites worldwide)

TO VISIT BEFORE YOU DIE BECAUSE

Enter through this Futuro Pod's aeroplane hatch to find out about life in a UFO-inspired house, reminiscent of a flying saucer.

The Futuro House by the Finnish architect Matti Suuronen (1933–2013) perfectly illustrates the post-war quest for a modular, prefabricated style of building, preferably one with an organic form. Suuronen's 1968 concept for a dwelling is a transportable fibreglass structure, inspired by a flying saucer, and is typical of the Space Age. The lightweight home was easy to replicate, buildable within a day, and transportable; it could even be relocated by helicopter. A Futuro House was equipped with a basic kitchen, bathroom, two bedrooms, and a sitting area. And thanks to the adjustable 'legs', the Futuro House was able to stand on uneven surfaces, such as mountainous terrain. The Finnish company Polykem produced a total of about six hundred models. But as a (holiday) home for private individuals, the Futuro House never really caught on, partly because the unit price was too high. The oil crisis in the early 1970s was detrimental to plastic design, including the Futuro House. But if utopian UFO-style homes tickle your fancy, you can find out more by visiting museums such as the Boijmans Van Beuningen Museum in Rotterdam or artist Craig Barnes', as pictured, which lands in different locations.

www.thefuturohouse.com

Europe  Finland

## 77 HVITTRÄSK (1903)

By Gesellius, Lindgren & Saarinen
Hvitträskintie 166, 02440 Luoma, Finland

**TO VISIT BEFORE YOU DIE BECAUSE**

A great example of national romantic architecture, this house epitomises Scandinavian design.

Finland also had its own version of Art Nouveau, known as the 'National Romantic Style'. Although it tends to lack the elegance of Belgian or French Art Nouveau, the 'nationalistic style' unleashed an architecture and design revolution in the Scandinavian countries. Inspiration came more from medieval architecture and age-old myths and legends than from the plant or animal world. The most intact example of that 'National Romantic Style' is Hvitträsk: the studio-home of the Finnish architectural firm Gesellius, Lindgren & Saarinen. They were responsible for the 'National Museum of Finland' in Helsinki and for the Finnish pavilion at the Paris World Exhibition in 1900. The house, some 30 kilometres outside Helsinki, later became the private home of Eliel Saarinen, the architect who emigrated to America in 1923 and established the reputation of Cranbrook Academy of Art. Those who visit Hvitträsk should definitely take the time to view the surrounding English garden. A walk by the other Art Nouveau villas around Lake Vitträsk is also highly recommended, although they are not open to the public.

Europe  Finland

# 78 VILLA MAIREA (1939)

By Alvar and Aino Aalto
Pikkukoivukuja 20, Noormarkku, Finland

TO VISIT
BEFORE YOU DIE
BECAUSE

This house located on a Finnish woodland site displays the perfect balance between Modernism and nature.

For Alvar Aalto (1898–1976), the forward-thinking Harry and Maire Gullichsen were dream clients. The entrepreneurs were not only the co-founders of furniture company Artek, for which Aalto created numerous designs; they were also his friends. They commissioned the Finnish architect to design an innovative summer house in a woodland site. Even though they were closely involved in guiding the final design, Aalto surprised them with an experimental structure that seamlessly unites the outer and the inner worlds. With a little imagination, when you step inside Villa Mairea, it feels like being inside a tree house, with the benefits of modern comforts. Aalto steered away from efficient functionalism, opting instead for a warm, 'organic' formal language that clearly hints at the influence of Frank Lloyd Wright and Japanese architecture. On the inside, the house strikes a perfect middle ground between modernism and nature, thanks to the input of Alvar's wife Aino. Aalto originally designed the famous Artek 'Tea Trolley 900', now a Finnish design classic, for this house.

www.villamairea.fi/en

Europe  Finland

# 79 MUURATSALO EXPERIMENTAL HOUSE (1953)

By Alvar Aalto
Melalammentie 2, 40900 Jyväskylä, Finland

**TO VISIT BEFORE YOU DIE BECAUSE**

Take in views of Lake Päijänne from this house which was constructed with 50 different types of brick and ceramic tile.

Of all the movements within modernism, the Scandinavian style is the most emotional, the most organic, and the warmest. Alvar Aalto (1898–1976) became the godfather of Finnish modernism, both in terms of architecture and product design. While experimenting, he developed a singular language, rooted in his love of nature. The most extreme example of his exploration of materials and textures is this playful 'Experimental House' of 1953. Shortly after the death of his wife Aino in 1949, he started designing a summer house for him and his second wife Elissa near Lake Päijänne. The house was one large laboratory: for instance, Aalto used more than fifty different types of brick, which he had arranged in different shapes and patterns. The house also has an innovative floor plan: it was conceived as a Roman atrium with a fire pit in the courtyard.

www.alvaraalto.fi/en/location/muuratsalo-experimental-house/

Europe     France

# 80   LE CABANON (1951–1952)

By Le Corbusier
Promenade Le Corbusier,
06190 Roquebrune-Cap-Martin, France

**TO VISIT BEFORE YOU DIE BECAUSE**

This rustic cabin embodies the quintessence of minimal, modern living.

Le Corbusier (1887 - 1965) was familiar with Roquebrune-Cap-Martin, where he stayed several times in Eileen Gray's home, E-1027. He built a log cabin just a stone's throw away, whose dimensions were in keeping with the 'Modulor' and occupied a square surface area of 3.66 metres on the ground and reaching a height of 2.26 metres. The 'Cabanon' is the embodiment of the mythical hut coupled with the precepts of modern architecture. The interior design is rustic and is reduced to the bare minimum: an entrance corridor with toilet facilities on the side and a single volume containing two single beds, a table, and a washbasin. It was an austere habitat suited to the life of a hermit, and Le Corbusier liked to stay here in the summer. The richness of the site undoubtedly lies in the garden and the Mediterranean below. Le Corbusier would go for a bathe there every morning until 27 August 1965, when he died after taking a swim.

www.capmoderne.com/en/lieu/le-cabanon/

Europe — France

# 81 HÔTEL MARTEL (1926–1927)

By Robert Mallet-Stevens
10 Rue Mallet-Stevens, M° Jasmin, 16ème arrondissement, Paris, France

**TO VISIT BEFORE YOU DIE BECAUSE**

Located in the street bearing the architect's name, this studio gave the Martel brothers the perfect work space for their sculptures.

The architect Robert Mallet-Stevens (1886–1945), one of the leading proponents of Modernism in France, built this remarkable studio with apartments for the sculptors and twin brothers Jan and Joël Martel. Located in the prestigious Rue Mallet-Stevens in Paris, it is one of five buildings that the architect built on this street. In addition to three self-contained apartments, the development includes a large studio set on two levels, with ceilings high enough to accommodate the sculptors' works. The studio is the main space in the house and is arranged on different levels, offering multiple perspectives. The façade is sculptural, with its white cubic masses, its recessed terraces, and an imposing cylindrical volume that encloses the circular staircase going up to the roof terrace. In front of the house, one might imagine that the luminous fountain designed by the architect had always been there. In fact it was placed there by the current owner only recently and was originally intended for the garden of the Casino de Saint-Jean de Luz.

Europe    France

## 82 LOUIS CARRÉ HOUSE (1957–1960)

By Elissa and Alvar Aalto
2 Chemin du Saint-Sacrement, 78490 Bazoches-sur-Guyonne, France

TO VISIT BEFORE YOU DIE BECAUSE

Pure lines, sumptuous detail, and sophisticated lighting make this house a sensual model for the Nordic way of life in France.

The modern art collector and gallery owner Louis Carré wanted to build a modern villa to house his collection on a hill in the Yvelines, to the southwest of Paris. Though he knew Le Corbusier and the rigour of his approach, he preferred the less radical style and the Finnish designs of Alvar Aalto (1898–1976), who was still little known in France at the time. He made a few simple demands: a slate roof to remind him of his native Brittany, and living rooms capable of housing his collections. The interior spaces are remarkably fluid and perfectly lit, by natural light and by Aalto's sophisticated lighting designs, with plenty of lamps to enhance all the rooms. Typical of Aalto's architecture, the lines are pure and the details meticulous, including the leather door handles, the claustra, and the ceilings. The latter were made of wood cut from a variety of different species, including oak, ash, pine, and beech, together providing a natural polychromy.

Europe — France

# 83 MAISONS LA ROCHE-JEANNERET (1923)

By Le Corbusier
8-10 Square du Docteur Blanche, 75016 Paris, France

**TO VISIT BEFORE YOU DIE BECAUSE**

Visiting this house will help you to understand the concept of the 'architectural promenade'.

These two semi-detached houses respond to very different agendas. One, the Jeanneret house, was built for Albert Jeanneret (Le Corbusier's brother), his wife, and two children. The other, the La Roche house, was intended for a bachelor – Raoul La Roche – who was passionate about modern art and a collector of mainly Cubist painters: Braque, Picasso, and Léger. The living spaces are grouped together on the same strip of land, while the gallery that houses the collection stands on stilts at the end of a Parisian dead end. The La Roche house is the embodiment of the architectural promenade, a concept dear to the architect: 'It is by walking, by moving around, that we see the ordinances of architecture develop,' Le Corbusier (1887 - 1965) once said. From the entrance, you begin a journey through a variety of perspectives, punctuated by plays of light, transparency, and openings to the world outside. The use of white, the dominant colour of modern architecture, is enhanced by the contrasts with the first attempts at polychromy, with blue and red arranged here and there to erase or affirm certain volumes in the house.

www.fondationlecorbusier.fr

Europe          France

# 84 MAISON UNAL (1973–2008)

By Claude Costy
Construction and Development by Joël Unal
07120 Labeaume, Ardèche, France

TO VISIT BEFORE YOU DIE BECAUSE

This house is like a poem, one recited at the heart of nature.

Situated in the heart of a forest in the Ardèche, this bubble house belongs to the realm of architecture-sculpture. It represents the realisation of a dream for Joël Unal and his wife, who lived in Grenoble in the 1970s and dreamt of a private home far away from the hustle and bustle of the city… and far away from the right angle. They fell under the spell of the works of Claude Costy, a pioneering architect in the field of architecture-sculpture. He drew up plans for the Unal house and, for the first time, his client was the builder. With no experience whatsoever, the Unals wanted to build their house themselves, extending the lifetime of the building site. They started in 1972 – when Joël Unal was 30 years old – and finished the construction in 2008. As the work progressed, Joël Unal appropriated the architects' plans, making changes according to the family's lifestyle, but also making additions - such as the swimming pool, which he built 25 years after construction first started.

The rounded forms of the house certainly help to give a sense of the quest for the freedom of the hippie and psychedelic period of the 1970s. The primary reason for the Unals pursuing this choice of the bubble house is the poetry of the round, organic form, as found in nature. The other determining factor is the economy of means, with the sphere being the most economical natural form, both in terms of materials and energy.

The bubbles are made using a technique for making unmoulded concrete walls, which are laid by hand on a metal armature. Joël Unal defines himself as a 'ferraillologue' or 'scrap metal specialist', having patiently sculpted every square centimetre of his house. The bubbles are painted white, which is not just chosen on aesthetic grounds, but also because it allows the house to remain 4 °C cooler. A cistern has been built to collect rainwater, as well as a swimming pool of the same capacity. Out of ecological considerations, the water stored in the winter is used to fill it up in the summer. With an eye on achieving a free and open way of life, the house has no interior partitions. The rooms are linked together in one continuous movement, set off by the orange-pink colour of the walls that unifies the whole ensemble. The furniture was integrated during the construction of the walls, with tables, shelves, and even a hammock made of concrete. The house becomes a shell, a nest. The forms open up and stretch out, in a long, sliding embrace.

Europe     France

# 85   PALACIO DE ABRAXAS (1978–1983)

By Ricardo Boffil
6 Place des Fédérés, 93160 Noisy-le-Grand, France

**TO VISIT BEFORE YOU DIE BECAUSE**

To fully understand Postmodernism and its references, a trip to the Abraxas Ensemble is a must.

Since the 1970s, the Catalan architect Ricardo Bofill (1939) has been engaged in defiance of 'mass architecture' and 'architecture by engineers without identity' – typified by the endless array of so many identical housing blocks – and has sought instead to create spaces for the people. Located near Paris, the Abraxas Ensemble is an application of Postmodernism, which calls for a return to classical Greek and Roman order (columns with a capital on top, pediments, and gigantism), and to symmetry and ornamentation. The very name Abraxas is a term from Greek gnosticism.

The monumental complex of 47,000 m$^2$ is comprised of 600 dwellings divided into three buildings, each referring to an element from classical antiquity:
— the Palacio, which is a colossal 18-storey building, neo-Greek in inspiration;
— the Theatre, which is arranged in a semi-circle that curves around a square built on the model of the ancient theatre, with columns that reflect the orders of classical Greek and Roman architecture;
— the Arch at the centre of it all, which is composed of two stairwells that are joined together at the top to form an arch.

www.lesdecouvreurs.com/produit/visite-guidee-espaces-abraxas-noisy-le-grand/

Europe — France

## 86 POSTMAN CHEVAL'S IDEAL PALACE (1879–1912)

By Joseph Ferdinand Cheval
8 rue du Palais, CS 10008, 26390 Hauterives, Drôme, France

**TO VISIT BEFORE YOU DIE BECAUSE**

Representing a lifetime's obsession for Cheval, this house is an ode to naivety.

This fascinating work of art brut or outsider's art produced by self-taught or naïve art makers – is unclassifiable. It leads us into the dreams of a postman who wanted to build his 'ideal palace', a sort of amalgamation of monuments from all countries and all eras: pagodas, caves, Egyptian and Hindu temples, the Swiss chalet, the mosque, and the medieval castle. This architectural curiosity is populated by an imaginary bestiary composed of deer, octopuses, bears, crocodiles, and elephants... but also fairies and mythological characters. The story begins in 1879 when the postman Ferdinand Cheval (1836 - 1924) was doing his daily rounds in the countryside. He stumbled upon an amazing rock that was to awaken his fantasy: to build the palace of his dreams, stone by stone, in the heart of his garden. Over a period of more than 30 years, he built each element of his palace from the shells, snails, stones, and oysters that he collected on his walks and assembled with lime mortar and cement. In a world of its own, and divorced from any kind of architectural context whatsoever, this ode to naivety is unique and full of poetry.

www.facteurcheval.com

Europe  France

## 87 RÉSIDENCE LE POINT DU JOUR (1958–1963)

By Fernand Pouillon and Jacques Henri Labourdette
1-10 Cours des Longs Prés, 92100 Boulogne-Billancourt, France

**TO VISIT BEFORE YOU DIE BECAUSE**

This house proves you can successfully combine aesthetics with social housing.

Fernand Pouillon (1912–1986) was one of the great builders in the reconstruction that took place in France after the end of World War II. He built a number of public buildings in Marseille and in the region of Paris, as well as in Algeria and Iran. His creations are characterised by the way they integrate with the site, the balance in the masses, the use of noble materials (even in social housing), and a willingness to collaborate with sculptors, ceramicists, and landscape artists. Located on the banks of the Seine on a plot of land that was formerly home to a number of old factories making car engines, this residence consists of 25 buildings with more than 2200 dwellings. The housing bears witness to the architect's desire to offer beauty to everyone, allowing harmony to reign between buildings and nature. Pouillon always sought to build the best possible works at the lowest possible cost, through the use of repeatable elements: 'This was as close as I ever got to achieving a programme that matched my ideal,' he once said.

https://destination.hauts-de-seine.fr/visite-guidee-residence-fernand-pouillon-boulogne-billancourt-hauts-de-seine.html

Europe — France

## 88 PRIVATE RESIDENCE OF JEAN PROUVÉ (1954)

By Jean Prouvé
4-6 Rue Augustin Hacquard, 54000 Nancy, France

**TO VISIT BEFORE YOU DIE BECAUSE**

This house was ahead of its time in using recycled materials in architecture.

Following the closure of his business in Paris, Jean Prouvé (1901–1984) decided to build himself a home using materials from unfinished projects. He bought a cheap piece of land on the side of a hill overlooking the city of Nancy, on a very steep slope thought impossible to build on. Built in a single summer, the house puts into practice the constructive principles of one of the most ingenious of modern architects and designers. The simplicity of its design, the lightness of the materials, and the speed of the assembly were all made possible by the use of prefabricated elements. Due to the sharp incline of the plot, the materials had to be brought in mostly by hand, or at best with a small truck, a restriction which demanded the use of light materials such as aluminium. Prouvé transferred technology from the world of industrial manufacturing to that of architecture, without abandoning any of its aesthetic qualities. In the garden below is the old office that he designed for his Ateliers de Maxéville in 1947.

Europe — France

# 89 THE 'RADIANT CITY' HOUSING UNIT (1946–1952)

By Le Corbusier
280 Boulevard Michelet, 13008 Marseille, France

**TO VISIT BEFORE YOU DIE BECAUSE**

Nestled between the hills and the Mediterranean, these housing units offer a breathtaking view from their roof terrace.

Designed to rehouse the victims of the districts destroyed by the war, this project was the first commission entrusted to Le Corbusier (1887 - 1965) by the French state. The unprecedented scale of the project was slowed down by budgetary problems and it ended up taking five years to complete instead of the twelve months initially envisaged. A veritable village on stilts, it contains everything needed to lead a self-contained and self-sufficient life, containing 337 dwellings, interior streets, shops, and a hotel-restaurant. On the roof terrace – which resembles the kind of transatlantic bridge that had inspired the architect over a period of 30 years – there is a crèche, a pool, and a sports hall. As the first development to apply the Modulor system, the unit also features some of the earliest sightings of industrialised furniture. With its exposed concrete framework, it laid the foundations for Brutalism in architecture. Le Corbusier dreamt of multiplying his units across neighbouring districts, but after several failures, he had to be content with building them in isolation, in Nantes-Rezé, Briey-en-Forêt, and Firminy.

www.fondationlecorbusier.fr

Europe — France

# 90 STUDIO-APARTMENT OF LE CORBUSIER (1934)

By Le Corbusier
24 Rue Nungesser et Coli, 75016 Paris, France

**TO VISIT BEFORE YOU DIE BECAUSE**

Gain access to the intimate living and working space of the master of Modernism.

With a surface area of some 240 m2, this studio-apartment is located on the seventh and eighth floors of the Molitor building that Le Corbusier (1887 - 1965) designed with his cousin Pierre Jeanneret (1896 - 1967) in 1934, and serves as a manifesto for his architectural thinking. He lived there with his wife, the former model Yvonne Gallis, from 1934 to 1965. The apartment has recently been restored to how it was in 1965, as testimony to the changes that Le Corbusier made in his living and working environment. No one was allowed to enter his studio, not even his wife. This is where he wrote his books and where he painted. In the whiteness of the dining room, the eye is drawn to a colourful stained-glass nook affixed to the window. This was a feature that Le Corbusier liked to build into his own home and the homes of others, as a little place to put personal belongings. On the first floor, a guest room opens out onto the rooftop garden, ideally placed to enjoy the light and the purest air, while avoiding the noise of the street.

www.fondationlecorbusier.fr

Europe — France

# 91 STUDIO-HOME OF THEO VAN DOESBURG (1930)

By Theo van Doesburg
29 Rue Charles Infroit, 92190 Meudon, France

**TO VISIT BEFORE YOU DIE BECAUSE**

See the live-work space of the most famous artists of the inter-war period.

The founder of the De Stijl movement, Dutch artist Theo van Doesburg (1883–1931), designed his studio-home near Paris for himself and his wife Nelly. It integrates the fundamental principles that emerged from his research on the cohesion of the plastic arts. The composition is minimal, consisting of two interlocking cubes, one for the house and the other for the studio, built overlooking the garden and dressed in a huge glass frame. Van Doesburg designed the house in its entirety: from the joinery, the stairs, the removable partitions, and the glass canopies, right down to the choice of both the flooring and the colours used for the stained glass. He died before the work was completed, and it was his wife who applied the colours to the front façade, as set out in his sketches. The woodwork is painted with the three primary colours dear to neoplasticism - blue, yellow, and red - contributing to the rhythm of the house. As a tribute to Theo and Nelly, the studio-home became the headquarters of the Van Doesburg House Foundation, which welcomes artists in residence.

www.vandoesburghuis.com

Europe — France

## 92 VILLA CAVROIS (1929–1932)

By Robert Mallet-Stevens
60 Avenue du Président John Fitzgerald Kennedy, 59170 Croix, France

TO VISIT BEFORE YOU DIE BECAUSE

Be amazed by a cinematic, sophisticated, and luxurious modern château.

The Parisian architect Robert Mallet-Stevens (1886–1945) was commissioned to design the Villa Cavrois by the wealthy textiles manufacturer Paul Cavrois. This family residence condenses all the state-of-the-art technologies of the time into high-quality luxury materials. There was nothing predetermined, however, about the Cavrois couple commissioning such a villa: they were not collectors, nor did they have any links to avant-garde circles. But Paul Cavrois dreamt of creating what no industrialist in the North had yet imagined: a modern house. The interior design is conceived as a cinematographic filmset, inspired by the sets from Marcel L'Herbier's film *Le Vertige* (1926), which Mallet-Stevens had designed. With all the different varieties of wood, the green and yellow marble, and the murals in ultramarine blue and lemon yellow, polychromy simply invades the spaces and amplifies the plastic modulations of the furniture and the décor. All the latest modern technology of the time is there: a telephone, a wireless, and a clock appear in every room. Outside, along the length of the 'cruiseliner', the magnificence of the building is dramatically heightened by the mirroring effect of the swimming pool. After a long period in which it was subject to vandalism and neglect, the state bought the villa in 2001 and restored it to show it off in all its glory.

Europe France

## 93 VILLA E-1027 (1926–1929)

By Eileen Gray and Jean Badovici
E-1027 Sentier Massolin, 06190 Roquebrune-Cap-Martin, France

TO VISIT
BEFORE YOU DIE
BECAUSE

This villa serves as a manifesto for Modernist architecture in the Mediterranean.

It is a strange name for a dream house, but one derived from the coded interweaving of the names of its two architects, Eileen Gray (1878–1976) and her husband Jean Badovici (1893–1956). The E is for Eileen, the 10 is for the J of Jean (since J is the tenth letter of the alphabet), the 2 is for the B of Badovici, and the 7 for the G of Gray. This was Eileen Gray's first architectural creation, and it testifies to her taste for and attention to detail. Over a period of three years, she designed each element of the furniture to embody its functional spirit, favouring mobile and inventive furniture, because, as she said, everyone 'has to be able to remain free and independent'. Accessible only via a path, the house has intimacy that extended by the seaside garden. Le Corbusier stayed at the villa to paint colourful murals in 1938, at a time when Eileen Gray was away. Some of these paintings represented naked figures, in an echo of his summertime practice of naturism. This proved to be a subject of discord with Eileen Gray, who did not appreciate his paintings, which she saw as being degrading within the immaculate white surroundings of her creation.

www.capmoderne.com/en/lieu/la-villa-e-1027/

Europe — France

# 94 VILLA FALBALA (1967–1969)

By Jean Dubuffet
Sentier des Vaux, 94520 Périgny-sur-Yerres, France

TO VISIT BEFORE YOU DIE BECAUSE

Complete with a 'philosophical exercise room', this house can open doors to your subconscious.

The Villa Falbala is the first part of the Closerie Falbala, a monumental work some 1610 m² in size that was created by the artist Jean Dubuffet (1901 - 1985). Built using epoxy resin and paint on sprayed concrete, this astonishing ensemble is comprised of a sort of garden surrounded by walls, with the Villa Falbala at its centre, a windowless house containing the Cabinet Lologique, which was intended to be the artist's 'philosophical exercise room', a sort of mecca for the mind. A major work from Jean Dubuffet's Hourloupe period, the villa is composed of walls and ceilings covered with hatched abstract forms in white, red, and blue. The artist was inspired by the automatic doodles that we draw when we are on the phone, or at a boring meeting, when our minds are totally distracted. 'The floor, which is itself also sculpted and painted, similarly evokes not a landscape, strictly speaking, but the mental and schematic figuration of a landscape,' he once said. 'Such that one feels, in this site, the impression of no longer being in nature, but in a mental interpretation of it.'

www.dubuffetfondation.com/

Europe   France

## 95 VILLA MAJORELLE (1902)

By Henri Sauvage (with Louis Majorelle)
1 Rue Louis Majorelle, 5400 Nancy, France

TO VISIT
BEFORE YOU DIE
BECAUSE

Behold the the most beautiful example of Art Nouveau from the Nancy school.

Henri Sauvage (1873–1932) was commissioned to build the Villa Majorelle for Louis Majorelle and his wife. Marjorelle was the Art Nouveau cabinetmaker and decorator from the Nancy school. Sauvage stood out as one of the rare architects of his generation prepared to constantly refresh his formal language. Like many industrialists in Nancy, Louis Majorelle situated his villa in the same street as his business. A successful marriage between architecture and organic Art Nouveau decoration, it is both elegant and luminous. The interior design was taken care of by an assortment of Art Nouveau artists, including Jacques Grüber, who produced the floral, stained-glass windows. Majorelle himself designed most of the furniture and the ironwork, particularly the elm-branch motifs that delicately support the awning over the entrance. He set up his vast studio on the third floor of the villa, under the gabled roof lit by a sumptuous arched bay with a vegetal design. Louis' wife gave birth to their only son, Jacques Majorelle, who later settled in Marrakech (see pp. 10 - 13).

www.musee-ecole-de-nancy.nancy.fr

Europe — France

## 96 VILLA ON THE ROCKS (2006)

By Rudy Ricciotti
Bandol, Provence-Alpes-Côte d'Azur, France

**TO VISIT BEFORE YOU DIE BECAUSE**

Take a dip in the spectacular (and unique) 28 metre aquarium pool which boasts transparent walls that look into the lower floor of this house.

The architect Rudy Ricciotti (1952) is known for his radical, creative architecture that gives pride of place to the innovative use of concrete. He built this house in his sunny hometown of Bandol, in the south of France. As with all his designs, the architect adapted this one to suit the terrain, with the line of the slope and the rock on which it is set providing its unique shape. Situated among the umbrella pines, at the heart of nature, the house blends traditional and modern materials. With its transparent walls, the most spectacular room is unquestionably the swimming pool, which is located in the centre of the house. On the intermediate level is a dormitory with transparent walls overlooking the pool. Offering multiple views, the house allows the light to filter through the large bay windows, which contrast with the roughness of the stone. 'All my villas disappear into the belly of the Earth,' said Ricciotti. You can rent the house to live the experience.

www.airbnb.com/rooms/15276929

Europe — France

## 97 VILLA NOAILLES (1925–1933)

By Robert Mallet-Stevens
Centre d'art d'intérêt national, Métropole Toulon Provence Méditerranée, Montée Noailles, 83400 Hyères, France

TO VISIT BEFORE YOU DIE BECAUSE

A legendary art and design project, this Modernist house is an intricate game of cubes and light.

The Viscount and Viscountess de Noailles were a fascinating patron couple who were in close contact with the French artistic avant-garde and regularly invited its practitioners to stay at their villa. For their holiday home, they turned to Robert Mallet-Stevens (1886 - 1945), a young architect still fairly new to the sector, who was better known at the time for his film sets. This commission was an opportunity for him to express the full range of his creativity, and it was to help him gain access to prestigious projects such as the Villa Cavrois. It was originally intended to be a relatively modest house built on a piece of land in the heights of Hyères that had been inherited as a wedding present. In the end, the project was extended, through multiple extensions, to include some 60 rooms across an area of 2000 m$^2$ – with gymnasium, squash court, and indoor swimming pool – the first such example in France. The interior design called upon the most renowned artists of the time, including Marcel Breuer, Eileen Gray, Sonia Delaunay, Raoul Dufy, and Giacometti. Today, Villa Noailles is an arts centre that presents exhibitions on architecture, fashion, photography, and design.

www.hyeres-tourisme.com/patrimoine-culturel/villa-noailles/

Europe — France

# 98 VILLA SAVOYE (1928–1931)

By Le Corbusier
82 Rue de Villiers, 78300 Poissy, France

**TO VISIT BEFORE YOU DIE BECAUSE**

This modern take on a French country house is one of the most significant contributions to architecture in the 20th century.

The Villa Savoye constitutes a manifesto for architecture's 'mouvement moderne'. In 1928, Pierre Savoye (the director of an insurance company) and his wife commissioned Le Corbusier (1887 - 1965) and Pierre Jeanneret (1896 - 1967) to design a country house near Paris. They applied to the letter the five essential points of modern architecture that Le Corbusier had set out in 1927: the free groundplan, the free façade, the *pilotis*, the horizontal windows, and the roof terrace. Like a white box suspended in the air, it seems powerful and serene in the midst of nature. Once inside, one reaches the first floor by a gentle slope, or via a majestic spiral staircase. Here, the rooms are arranged around a large glazed terrace, which erases the boundary between inside and outside, a feature that is typical of Le Corbusier. From the terrace-solarium, an outside ramp leads sensually to a hanging garden. Despite its undeniable aesthetic qualities, the construction was not well suited to the site or to the climate. After being put to various forms of use, the house came into the hands of the state, which initiated the procedure to give the building classified status in Le Corbusier's own lifetime.

www.villa-savoye.fr

Europe      Germany

# 99    HAUS AM HORN (1923)

By Georg Muche and Adolf Meyer
Am Horn 61, 99425 Weimar, Germany

**TO VISIT BEFORE YOU DIE BECAUSE**

Explore the first architectural creation of the Bauhaus, a prototype for affordable housing.

Haus am Horn was actually an experimental student project. Founded in 1919, the Bauhaus presented modern ideas first applied to architecture and interior design. Architect Georg Muche (1895 - 1987) and Adolf Meyer (1881 - 1929) designed a functionalist plan around a central living area, with little unnecessary detail or wasted surface area. The interior had fitted wardrobes and carpets, lamps, and furniture designed by Breuer and Moholy-Nagy, Bauhaus students at the time. Unfortunately, Haus am Horn never got further than a prototype. There were plans for a property development project in Weimar with several similar houses. However, due to inflation, only one model home was built: the Haus am Horn. Georg Muche and Adolf Meyer were responsible for the design and construction, under the watchful eye of then-Bauhaus director Walter Gropius. Haus am Horn has frequently changed owners, and has been severely damaged and restored several times. In 1996, it was added to the list of UNESCO World Heritage Sites. In Weimar itself, the model home belongs to an archipelago of special Bauhaus designs. The most recent addition, a brand-new museum, opened in 2019 to mark the centenary of the Bauhaus.

www.klassik-stiftung.de/en/the-foundation/our-profile/construction-projects/haus-am-horn/

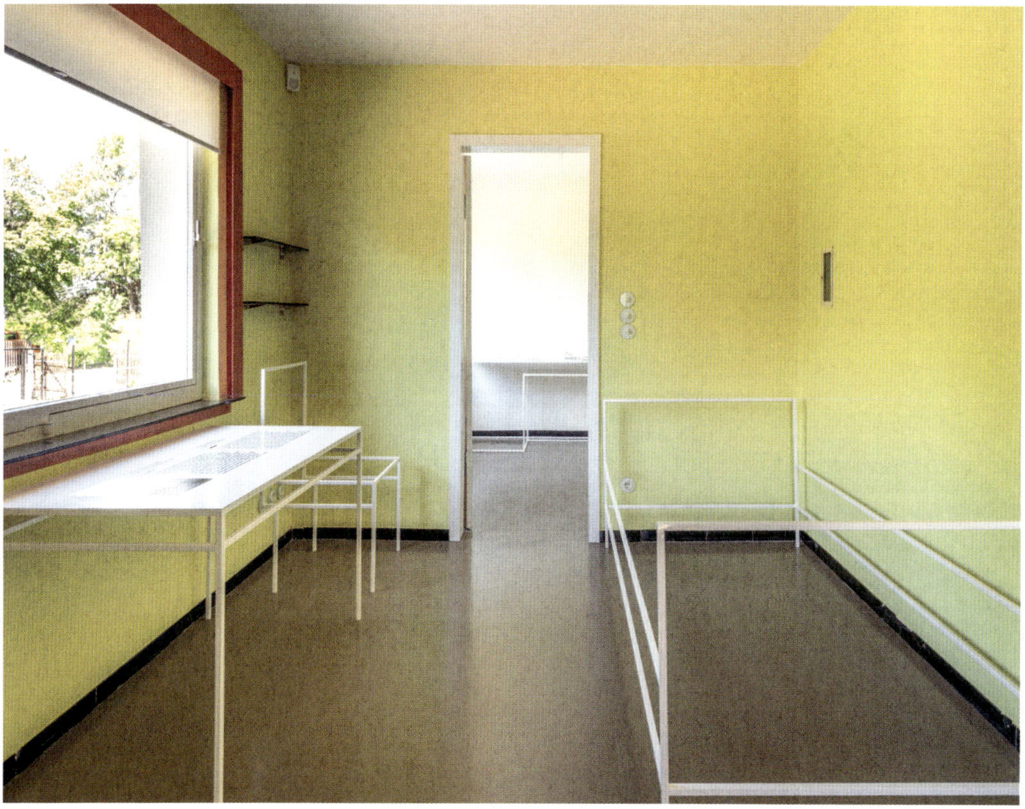

Europe  Germany

# 100 HAUS HOHE PAPPELN (1907–1908)

By Henry van de Velde
Belvederer Allee 58, 99425 Weimar, Germany

**TO VISIT BEFORE YOU DIE BECAUSE**

A 'total work of art' created by the spiritual father of the Bauhaus, this house is named after the slender poplar trees on the property.

The Hohe Pappeln villa in Weimar was the private home of the Belgian architect and designer Henry van de Velde (1863–1957). His family home, which dates from 1907–1908, is a total work of art, for which – just as in the Hohenhof in Hagen – he designed every detail: from furniture to fabrics, from ceramics to lighting. The name Hoge Pappeln refers to the slender poplars that Van de Velde found on the site. Weimar was the starting point of his German career. He moved there in 1899 and in 1901 became a 'creative' consultant to William Ernest, Grand Duke of Saxe-Weimar-Eisenach. Between 1904 and 1911 he built the School of Arts and Crafts, of which he became the first director. That school would eventually evolve into the Bauhaus in 1919. Van de Velde also co-founded the German Werkbund and was a crucial figure in the German Jugendstil. World War I meant that he and his family had to return to Belgium in 1917. The Hohe Pappeln house changed hands several times in the 20th century, until the Klassik Stiftung Weimar converted the building into a house museum in 2003, eventually owning the property since 2012.

www.klassik-stiftung.de/haus-hohe-pappeln/

Europe  Germany

# 101 HOHENHOF (1906–1908)

By Henry van de Velde
Stirnband 10, 58093 Hagen, Germany

TO VISIT BEFORE YOU DIE BECAUSE

Henry van de Velde's 'total work of art' symbolises an attempt to reform social life through art and design.

Although Henry van de Velde (1863–1957) is widely known as one of the founders of Art Nouveau in Belgium, the architect-designer evolved into a fully fledged modernist with an international reputation. In 1899 he settled in Weimar, Germany, where he founded the School of Arts and Crafts, the predecessor of the Bauhaus. Between 1906 and 1908 he built Hohenhof, the Art Nouveau private home of the visionary art collector Karl Ernst Osthaus (1874–1921). He founded the Folkwang Museum in 1902 and was convinced that good design and good architecture have the power to enhance the quality of life. The design for his private residence is in line with his attempt to transform the industrial city of Hagen into a garden city with superlative avant-garde architecture by figures such as Gropius, Behrens, and Riemerschmid. Unfortunately, the project stalled due to the outbreak of World War I. The Osthaus residence is a true 'total work of art'. Van de Velde also specially designed the wallpaper, furniture, crockery, and home textiles. The architect advised Osthaus, whose extensive collection includes work by Matisse, Hodler, and Vuillard, on integrating the artworks into the interior design.

www.osthausmuseum.de

Europe — Germany

# 102 HAUS LANGE AND HAUS ESTERS (1928–1930)

By Mies van der Rohe
Wilhelmshofallee 91-97, 47800 Krefeld, Germany

**TO VISIT BEFORE YOU DIE BECAUSE**

Modernism's most famous Siamese twins, these houses are celebrated for their dark red brick, characteristic flat roofs, and cuboids, inserted one inside the other.

Now in service as extramural exhibition spaces of Kunstmuseen Krefeld, in 1930 Haus Lange and Haus Esters were two adjoining houses, designed by Ludwig Mies van der Rohe (1886–1969). Although not identical, they share a similar design: brown brick façades supported by a steel structure. The clients, Josef Esters and Hermann Lange, were two industrialists from Krefeld. Haus Lange (1928) and Haus Esters (1930) are among the works that Mies realised at the pinnacle of his career in Europe: in 1929 he designed the Barcelona Pavilion, in 1930 he completed Villa Tugenthat in Brno. In 1930 the German architect became the last director of the Bauhaus. In 1933, several years before the outbreak of World War II, it was forced to close its doors. Frustrated by the Nazi action, Mies moved to the States, where he accepted a teaching assignment and was awarded several major assignments.

www.kunstmuseenkrefeld.de

*Europe*     *Germany*

# 103 HAUS UNGERS (1959)

By Oswald Mathias Ungers
Belvederestraße 60, 50933 Cologne, Germany

TO VISIT BEFORE YOU DIE BECAUSE

Home to one of the world's most important architectural libraries, this house is a complex interaction of differently defined volumes that together form a whole.

If you take a Brutalist architectural safari in Cologne, you must visit the concrete churches designed by Gottfried Böhm and Heinz Buchmann. Rolf Gutbrod's Corbusian university library is also worth the trip. But don't forget to visit Haus Ungers: the private home and design studio of architect Oswald Mathias Ungers (1926–2007). He was one of the most important architects of the Berlin reconstruction and completed the first version of his house in 1959. Thanks to its simple materials – concrete and red brick – it can justifiably be called Brutalist avant-la-lettre. The structure continued to evolve over the years, during which it served as a manifesto reflecting his ideas as they progressed. In 1989, Ungers added a grey block-shaped volume in basalt to his original home, which he devoted primarily to housing his vast library. With over 12,000 historical titles – including early editions of Palladio, Vitruvius, and Piranesi – this library forms the backbone of the Ungers Archive for Architectural Studies (UAA) foundation, which is now based in the building. Visits are by appointment only.

www.ungersarchiv.de/

Europe     Germany

# 104   VILLA STUCK (1897–1898)

By Franz von Stuck
Prinzregentenstraße 60, 81675 Munich, Germany

**TO VISIT BEFORE YOU DIE BECAUSE**

Munich's most eccentric *Gesamtkunstwerk*, Villa Stuck is celebrated as a marvellously modern, yet curious, construction.

With its Nazi past, Villa Stuck isn't Munich's most celebrated architectural monument. The private villa of the decadent German artist Franz von Stuck (1863–1928) – Hitler's favourite – deserves better. His artist's residence is a late 19th-century palace, its idiosyncratic interior designed by Von Stuck himself. He bridges the 19th and 20th centuries. As an artist, he was influenced by Symbolists such as Böcklin, but also taught modern artists including Paul Klee, Wassily Kandinsky, and Josef Albers. Von Stuck was a founder of the Munich Secession. Like the more famous Wiener Secession, it championed cross-pollination between free art forms (architecture, painting, music, theatre, opera) and applied art. Villa Stuck is the pinnacle of this ambition: a bombastic stand-alone work of art, overflowing with lavish materials and decorative references to Classical antiquity, Byzantium, and the Renaissance, complemented by ideas from the emerging Art Nouveau movement. Here, Von Stuck ventured into wallpaper and trompe-l'œil murals, as well as furniture design, with which he won a gold medal at the 1900 Paris World Exhibition. Thanks to the efforts of patrons such as Hans Joachim and Amélie Ziersch, Villa Stuck has been a museum since 1992.

www.villastuck.de

Europe  Germany

# 105 MASTERS' HOUSES (1925–1926)

By Walter Gropius
Ebertallee 59-71, 06846 Dessau-Roßlau, Germany

**TO VISIT BEFORE YOU DIE BECAUSE**

See how Bauhaus teachers such as Klee and Kandinsky lived in these semi-detached houses considered prototypes of 'white modernism'.

For Bauhaus enthusiasts, Dessau is a UNESCO protected pilgrimage site. Within walking distance of the Bauhaus School building in Dessau are the Masters' Houses: a cluster of four dwellings built between 1925 and 1926 by Walter Gropius (1883–1969). The three semi-open houses share the same floor plan, but the director's house was conceived differently. Gropius designed his Masters' Houses as prototypes that exemplify his ideas of modern and functional living. Originally, the houses were designed for teachers and directors of the Bauhaus. Gropius, Schlemmer, Feiniger, Stölz, Moholy-Nagy, Albers, Klee, Kandinsky: the list of residents reads like a *Who's Who* of the Bauhaus. The architect literally conceived the houses as a construction kit: true to the Bauhaus philosophy, he designed a structure comprising modular, prefabricated elements, which allowed uniformity and standardisation. In 1933, the Bauhaus was forced to close, and the Masters' Houses were severely damaged during the Nazi regime and World War II. The three identical houses have since been restored, and the director's house was reinterpreted in 2014 by the architectural firm of Bruno Fioretti Marquez.

Europe — Germany

# 106 SCHMINKE HOUSE (1933)

By Hans Scharoun
Kirschallee 1B, 02708 Löbau, Germany

**TO VISIT BEFORE YOU DIE BECAUSE**

The curved body, terraces, outside stairs, and porthole-shaped windows make this the most sensual 'steamship' villa on the planet.

In 1933 Hans Scharoun (1893–1972) built a unique home for noodle factory owner Fritz Schminke. Despite the rise of Nazi ideology in Germany, the modernist house in Löbau retained its timeless iconic value and continues to inspire new generations of architects. The projecting façades, external staircase, porthole windows, and spacious terraces instantly evoke a ship, a metaphor that inspired numerous architects in the interbellum period. The house also reaches out to its surroundings: the undulating lines of the architecture merge seamlessly with the flowing garden. After World War II, the family home had a rather turbulent history. It was occupied on several occasions by very different organisations, including the Russian Army and a communist youth movement FDJ. The home is now owned by a foundation. After the war, Scharoun earned a reputation for designing major public buildings, including the concert hall of the Berliner Philharmoniker (1963).

www.stiftung-hausschminke.eu/

Europe        Germany

# 107 WEISSENHOFSIEDLUNG (1927)

By Le Corbusier and others
Rathenaustrasse 1-3, 70191 Stuttgart, Germany

**TO VISIT BEFORE YOU DIE BECAUSE**

This neighbourhood is an all-star cluster of outstanding modernist architecture now preserved as a museum.

The Weißenhofsiedlung residential area in Stuttgart, which dates from 1927, is one of the most important clusters of modernist architecture in Europe. Commissioned by the city of Stuttgart, Mies van der Rohe selected 17 architects to design an estate with modern terraced houses and apartment blocks for people from lower income groups. The architect supervised their plans and the construction process. Although Le Corbusier and Pierre Jeanneret, Peter Behrens, Victor Bourgeois, Josef Frank, Walter Gropius, Mies van der Rohe, Hans Scharoun, Mart Stam, and Bruno Taut introduced their own idiosyncratic accents, the estate nonetheless displays a strong stylistic unity. Scharoun's house was distinctive for its curves, and Bruno Taut's house was the only one painted in red, yellow, and blue. There was a total of 21 dwellings, several of which, including Taut's design, were destroyed by air raids in World War II. It is now a UNESCO-protected site, and about ten of the houses are intact. When the estate was built, Van der Rohe and the Deutscher Werkbund allocated the largest budgets to Le Corbusier (1887 - 1965) and his cousin Pierre Jeanneret (1896 - 1967). And it is these two buildings on the Weißenhofsiedlung that can now be visited as a museum.

www.weissenhofmuseum.de

Europe — Germany

# 108 TAUT'S HAUS (1925)

By Bruno Taut
Gielower Strasse 43, 12359 Berlin, Germany

TO VISIT
BEFORE YOU DIE
BECAUSE

Stay a night in this Berlin Bauhaus gem to appreciate its strong genuine interior colours, clever room layouts, and characterful design details.

Although architecture tourism is in, there are very few modernist houses where you can spend the night. In the Hufeisensiedlung, a modernist housing project in Berlin, you can rent one of Bruno Taut's houses. Between 1925 and 1930, architect and urban planner Taut (1880–1938) designed a social housing development set in a green environment, which was awarded UNESCO World Heritage status in 2008. Behind the colourful façade of Taut's residence is a compact, highly functional family home; Katrin Lesser and Ben Buschfeld purchased the property, and funded its restoration. They also maintained Taut's bold colour scheme for the interior and decorated the house with Bauhaus-inspired furniture and art objects. Not only an architect, Bruno Taut was also a theorist and author. In 1919 he published a manifesto on the use of colour in architecture. As the chief architect of the Berlin public housing cooperative GEHAG, he designed several extremely colourful residential complexes. Between 1924 and 1931, he and his team built a total of around 12,000 homes. In 1933, as Nazism gained ground, he fled Germany, ultimately arriving in Japan where he lived until 1936, then relocating to Turkey (until his death in 1938).

www.tautes-heim.de/

Europe  Italy

# 109 CASA CRESPI (1938)

By Gabriela Crespi
Italy, Brera area

TO VISIT
BEFORE YOU DIE
BECAUSE

Traces of Crespi's exceptional life echo throughout her jet-set apartment.

Gabriela Crespi (1922–2017) was a unique voice among the Milanese design community because she consciously chose not to work for the industry, but only with artisans, and in limited editions. Her luxurious designs and glitzy interiors were largely inspired by nature. Yet her style is difficult to pin down: she designed bronze animal sculptures as well as bamboo furniture and brass coffee tables. Her life is equally fascinating: at the age of 65, she swapped her design career to embark upon a spiritual quest, became entranced by a guru, and spent 20 years living in India. In Milan she had an impeccably furnished apartment on the fourth floor of a 1930s apartment block in the Brera district. The guestbook reads like a *Who's Who* of the cultural and artistic world. Her personal belongings, furniture designs, travel souvenirs, collection of ceramics, and Chinese artefacts are in her apartment, just as she left them. The apartment still holds her entire archive of more than 2000 designs. Since Crespi's death, her daughter Elisabetta has begun to catalogue and digitise her work. Architecture-lovers can visit the gorgeously decorated apartment, but reservation is required.

www.gabriellacrespi.it/en/

Europe — Italy

## 110 CASA REMO BRINDISI (1971–1973)

By Nanda Vigo
Via Nicolò Pisano 45, 44029 Lido di Spina, Comacchio, Ferrara, Italy

**TO VISIT BEFORE YOU DIE BECAUSE**

This splendid and modern house museum of the painter Remo Brindisi looks like a Kubrickesque swimming pool.

On the coast of the Italian province of Ferrara, artist Remo Brindisi (1918–1996) commissioned an eccentric villa as a place where artists, friends, and art could meet. The painter / writer / set designer worked with Nanda Vigo (1936–2020), the eccentric Milanese architect whose experimental oeuvre – on the interface of architecture, sculpture, and installation – was recently rediscovered. Casa Remo Brindisi can be regarded as one huge experiment, in which life becomes a kind of theatre. The house was built at the height of Brindisi's career. He always intended the villa to be an exhibition space to display his impressive private collection, even in the bathrooms and toilets. And yet the architecture is a work of art in its own right. Vigo and Brindisi dressed each of the spaces in rectangular white tiles with dark grouting. Vigo disrupted that tight grid with a circular atrium from which a sculptural spiral staircase ascends. This feature makes the house seem like a cross between a swimming pool and a graphic backdrop for a Kubrick film. Brindisi took his last breath here in 1996. His own oeuvre has been somewhat forgotten, but he left us a completely unique 'mausoleum' that lives on, a vibrant tribute to art.

No official website

Europe    Italy

# 111 CASA SALDARINI (1962)

By Vittorio Giorgini
Via Vittorio Giorgini, Località Baratti, 57025 Piombino, Livorno, Italy

**TO VISIT BEFORE YOU DIE BECAUSE**

The house that looks like a whale was the first first building in the world based on an iso-elastic membrane made of concrete and wire netting.

Tuscany may be famous for its beautiful traditional country houses but, in the Gulf of Baratti, you'll find a Space Age abode that will fire your imagination. Casa Saldarini is sometimes referred to as Casa Dinosauro or 'The Whale', because of its zoomorphic curves. Florentine architect Vittorio Giorgini (1926–2010) designed it for Rino Saldarini in 1962. It was the first house ever built with an iso-elastic membrane over a mesh of reinforcing steel. With his organic design, Giorgini was working in the same genre as 1960s architects and product designers such as Antti Lovag, Jacques Couëlle, and Pascal Häusermann, who experimented with new modes of residential architecture in unorthodox materials and shapes. In 1969, the architect moved from his famous 'Hexagon House' in Tuscany to New York, where he taught at the Pratt Institute. His Casa Dinosauro is one of architectural history's forgotten masterpieces, and bears witness to a period of unfettered fantasy and belief in progress.

www.casadinosaurobaratti.com/en

Europe  Italy

## 112 VILLA BORSANI (1939–1944)

By Osvaldo Borsani
Via Umberto I, 148, 20814 Varedo, Province of Monza and Brianza, Italy

**TO VISIT BEFORE YOU DIE BECAUSE**

Although Borsani is world famous for his furniture, this house shows that he's also one of architecture's unsung heroes.

In 1953, Osvaldo Borsani (1911–1985) and his twin brother Fulgenzio launched the furniture brand Tecno. Architects such as Gae Aulenti and Norman Foster designed furniture for the company, as did Borsani himself. Although less renowned than his contemporaries Gio Ponti or Achille Castiglioni, he was a talented designer-architect, and merits equal attention. In 1933 he made his architectural debut with his 'Casa Minima': a compact functionalist house, with which he participated in the Milan Triennial. But, with its volumes, materials, and details, the villa that he designed for his twin brother between 1939 and 1944 epitomises his sophistication. Although rational in approach, the detailing is sumptuous. Since the death of Fulgenzio's widow, the villa in Varedo, some 30 kilometres from Milan, has been the property of the Archives Osvaldo Borsani. Naturally, Tecno furniture takes pride of place, but is accompanied by an abundance of antiques and several important interventions by artist Lucio Fontana, a friend of the Borsanis. But please, don't turn up at Via Umberto I 148 in Varedo unannounced: you have to make an appointment to visit the family villa.

www.osvaldoborsani.com/architettura/villa-varedo-1943

Europe — Italy

## 113 VILLA NECCHI-CAMPIGLIO (1932–1935)

By Piero Portaluppi
Via Mozart, 14, 20122 Milan, Italy

**TO VISIT BEFORE YOU DIE BECAUSE**

This villa provides the setting for the film *I Am Love* by the director Luca Guadagnino.

Nestled in the heart of a majestic Milanese garden lined with century-old magnolias, the Villa Necchi-Campiglio is a perfect example of the rigorous, monumental Art Deco architecture that was built for the bourgeoisie of Lombardy in the period between the wars. It was commissioned by Angelo Campiglio, his wife Gigina Necchi, and his sister-in-law Edda Necchi, the heirs to the Necchi sewing-machine factories, who called upon the rationalist architect Piero Portaluppi (1888 - 1967) to realise their dreams of a house at the cutting edge of modernity. Falsely austere, the villa blends luxury, monumentality, and elegance, in the way that only Italy can offer. Everything has been considered in terms of comfort and leisure, with facilities that are very avant-garde for the time, including integrated central heating, sliding doors, a heated swimming pool, a covered tennis court, and a projection room. The villa's Art Deco furnishings were partly designed by the architect and are enriched with paintings by De Chirico and Giorgio Morandi, and sculptures by Arturo Martini.

www.fondoambiente.it/luoghi/villa-necchi-campiglio

Europe　　　　　　　　　　Italy

# 114　VILLA LEONI (1941–1944)

By Pietro Lingeri
Via Provinciale, 2, 22010 Ossuccio, Como, Italy

**TO VISIT BEFORE YOU DIE BECAUSE**

The villa is a masterpiece created by an architect of Benito Mussolini's facist regime.

Villa Leoni in Ossuccio, a private residence from 1941 to 1944, was built for Diana Peduzzi and Raffaele Leoni, who were involved in the textile industry. The villa embodies the spirit of Italian rationalism on the eve of World War II. At that time, architecture in Italy was enjoying a heyday under Benito Mussolini. Many architects designed buildings in a stylistic modernist-nationalistic fusion, with echoes of ancient Rome paired with an exultant symmetry and monumentality. Pietro Lingeri (1894–1968), the architect of Villa Leoni, was one of rationalism's seminal figures. As a writer, he published articles in numerous magazines, helping to propagate the new style. He also worked closely with architect Giuseppe Terragni on various projects, such as the 'Casa del Fascio' in Como, commissioned by the fascist party. Lingeri also helped to design the unrealised 'Danteum': a monument in honour of Dante, intended for the World Exhibition in 1942 in Rome. Mussolini's idea of building an entire exhibition district failed. Villa Leoni was built in its entirety, and the lavish house can be rented for events and weddings. You can also pre-book a tour of the villa.

www.villaleonilocation.it/

Europe — Italy

# 115 VILLA OTTOLENGHI (1974–1978)

By Carlo Scarpa
Str. Scanelli, 5, 37011 Bardolino, Verona, Italy

**TO VISIT BEFORE YOU DIE BECAUSE**

This villa on the eastern shore of Lake Garda distils the quintessence of Scarpa's 1970s creativity.

The Villa Ottolenghi is one of the final creations by the Venetian architect Carlo Scarpa (1906 - 1978). Situated on sloping vineyards with multiple views of Lake Garda, it was designed for the lawyer Ottolenghi and his family. Scarpa had to adapt to the constraints of the site and to the city's urban planning regulations, which prohibited construction any higher than one floor above ground level. He consequently buried most of the space underground, thereby minimising the visual impact of the house in its natural environment. Access is obtained via a narrow passage – reminiscent of the streets of Venice – which leads from the road to the roof garden that serves as a terrace. The eye is drawn to the mineral and rustic aspect of the house, in which concrete is used in combination with glass, wood, natural stone, and forms of vegetation breaking through the surface. Largely influenced by Frank Lloyd Wright and by Japanese architecture, Scarpa created a series of ponds to mark a gentle separation between the interior and exterior.

No official website

Europe — The Netherlands

## 116 DIAGOON HOUSING (1971)

By Herman Hertzberger
Gebbenlaan 32, 2625 KB, Delft, The Netherlands

**TO VISIT BEFORE YOU DIE BECAUSE**

A polyvalent carcass with fixed functions, this house was to be completed, expanded, and filled in by the inhabitants themselves.

In the Netherlands, Herman Hertzberger (1932) and Aldo van Eyck are the most famous structuralist architects. Hertzberger's philosophy is unusual because he broke with the traditional straitjacket of the family home. He wanted to get away from standardisation in housing, and advocated giving the occupant more freedom. Instead of designing everything for the client, Hertzberger designed the home's structure and the quality of light as a semi-finished product. It is up to the residents to design the functions of the home according to their needs or habits. This means that you are able to choose the right place for each activity. The house can grow old along with its occupants, or can be adjusted again by the next residents according to their own needs and insights. This innovative vision is clearly expressed in Hertzberger's conceptual Diagoon Housing, designed between 1967 and 1969. Originally, the plan was to create an entire development of 324 units in Vaassen near Apeldoorn. However, because construction costs were high, only eight units were built as an experiment between 1970 and 1971 in the post-war neighbourhood Buitenhof in Delft. You can visit one of them by appointment, in groups of up to six people. A unique touch; your tour guide is the current resident, architect Robert von der Nahmer. He will show you around the Diagoon house complete with tower room, 'ship's ladder', and draw bridge to the roof terrace in the original 'Hertzberger' purple.

www.diagoonwoningdelft.nl

Europe — The Netherlands

# 117 JAN DE JONG HOUSE (1967–1968)

By Jan de Jong
Rijksweg 56, 5374 RB Schaijk, The Netherlands

**TO VISIT BEFORE YOU DIE BECAUSE**

Inspired by the architectonic style proposed by his teacher-monk, Jan de Jong equipped this unique house with the spiritual sanctity of a cloister.

The Jan de Jong House in Schaijk is a rare example of a private residence designed entirely in the Bossche School. This Dutch architectural movement was famed for its spiritual approach and austere formal language, based on well-defined proportions. Jan de Jong (1917-2001) was influenced by the monk-architect Dom Hans van der Laan, the theoretician of the Bossche School who trained De Jong in ecclesiastical architecture. You can see how these influences also shaped the private home and studio that De Jong designed for himself in the 1960s. Far from florid, the architecture breathes a distinct sense of quietude, timelessness, and intimacy. Coming to the house as a visitor, you are immediately humbled by the proportions, muted tones, and restrained palette of materials. De Jong sought to create a house that exuded a sacred atmosphere, with proportions based on Van der Laan's theory of the 'Plastic Number'. One of the structure's most remarkable elements is the use of columns to introduce spatial rhythm and to intuitively distinguish functions. The columns are also allusions to secular Roman architecture. In his pursuit of timeless architecture, De Jong tore down his own English country-house style home, which was built in 1949, to replace it with this plain L-shaped abode with a walled garden, both of which comply with all his principles.

www.hendrickdekeyser.nl/de-huizen/huis-jan-de-jong

Europe     The Netherlands

# 118   WALL HOUSE #2 (1973)

By John Hejduk
A.J. Lutulistraat 17, 9728 WT Groningen, The Netherlands

**TO VISIT BEFORE YOU DIE BECAUSE**

Hejduk's 1970s masterpiece fundamentally changed the concept of architecture and dwelling.

In the northern Dutch city of Groningen, you can find both the post-modern Groninger Museum (1994), and one of the most transformative houses in the history of the 20th century: Wall House #2. It was designed by John Hejduk (1929 – 2000), an American avant-garde architect and highly influential figure in the architecture and architectural education of the late 20th century. The house consists of a vast, seemingly free-standing concrete wall, 18.5 meters wide and 14 meters high. Suspended from it, like interconnected sculptures, are a series of biomorphically shaped residential units. It was the American landscape architect Ed Bye who commissioned Hejduk in 1973 for a private home in Ridgefield, Connecticut, not in Groningen. Unfortunately, due to the unforseen construction costs, Bye was forced to cancel the project. Thanks to John Hejduk's long standing relationship with the Netherlands – he was in close contact with the NAi and several Dutch architects and patrons - the house was finally built in Groningen in 2000-2001. The German architect Thomas Muller who was a close friend of Hejduk's assisted the city of Groningen as the project architect. In September 2001, the house opened during the city's annual Blue Moon Festival. The City of Groningen requested the Groninger Museum to manage Wall House #2, especially to ensure its public use and cultural designation.

# 119 SONNEVELD HOUSE (1933)

By Brinkman & Van der Vlugt
Jongkindstraat 12, 3015 CG Rotterdam, The Netherlands

**TO VISIT BEFORE YOU DIE BECAUSE**

This is the most beautifully preserved functionalist home in the Netherlands.

Built in 1933, Sonneveld House is a prime example of 'het nieuwe bouwen', the Dutch movement that was part of international modernism. The Rotterdam house was designed by Brinkman & Van der Vlugt, an architectural firm known for its functionalist designs, such as the Van Nelle Factory and the Feyenoord stadium. The villa is a *tour de force*, in both formal and technical terms. The heirs of the Rotterdam Sonneveld family supported the restoration of the house, and provided the researchers with key archival documents, as well as the original furniture and fittings from 1933. Although the villa has been home to other residents, the house was restored to its original state during the time of the Sonnevelds. A visit to this listed building allows you to experience what life must have been like in a functionalist house that features a surprising range of colour. Seeking to preserve the vitality of the villa, contemporary artists and designers are invited to create installations that respond to the Sonneveld House legacy, while respecting its authenticity.

Europe · The Netherlands

# 120 VAN SCHIJNDEL HOUSE (1992)

By Mart van Schijndel
Pieterskerkhof 8, 3512 JR Utrecht, The Netherlands

**TO VISIT BEFORE YOU DIE BECAUSE**

Van Schijndel devised unique glass doors with silicone sealant rather than hinges for this partially hidden private home in the old centre of Utrecht.

Few significant architectural houses from the 1990s are open to the public. But the Van Schijndel House, which architect Mart van Schijndel (1943–1999) designed for himself in Utrecht, is an interesting exception. It took him five years to invent the concept for his 'house of light and air', because the design was anything but conventional: he condensed his principal vision of volumes, light, space, and interior into a mere 175 m². For the inventive way in which he pulled this off, Van Schijndel was awarded the Rietveld Prize in 1995. The jury called his design 'virtuoso and sculptural'. In 1999, the year that Van Schijndel died, Utrecht added the architect's home to its list of monuments. There the house is considered on a par with the Rietveld Schröder House, the architectural masterpiece designed by Gerrit Rietveld. Perhaps the most striking detail is the glass doors, which have silicone adhesive seams instead of hinges. Another special feature is that Van Schijndel designed almost all of the bespoke interior elements. The property is still occupied, but can be visited (by confirmed appointment) every first Sunday of the month.

www.martvanschijndel.nl/

Europe  The Netherlands

# 121 KIEFHOEK RESIDENCE (1925–1930)

By J.J.P. Oud
Hendrik Idoplein 2, 3073 RC Rotterdam, The Netherlands

**TO VISIT BEFORE YOU DIE BECAUSE**

A serially produced 'machine' in which to live, this house uses a functionalist urban layout and ingenious ground plan to create a maximum living space.

Rotterdam boasts a fascinating cluster of modernist architecture. Several of these iconic private homes are open to visitors. As well as the Sonneveld House (Brinkman & Van der Vlugt, 1933), the Chabot Museum (G.W. Baas, 1938) and the Cube Houses (Piet Blom, 1984), you can visit the modernist Kiefhoek. Like the Weißenhofsiedlung, this is a residential area that was built in the interwar period when there was insufficient housing for working-class families. Architect J.J.P. Oud (1890–1963), one of the crucial figures in De Stijl, designed a master plan for some 300 family homes with extra facilities, such as shops and a water distillery. In 1930 the residential complex reached completion. A tour of the preserved and restored Kiefhoek house reveals Oud's ingenuity in designing these compact residences. The housing estate is the culmination of Oud's functionalist period, known as 'nieuwe zakelijkheid' or 'new objectivity', in which the house is approached as a serially produced 'machine'. To keep construction costs down, the architecture and furnishings were standardised wherever possible, yet Oud managed to create high-quality, smart houses with limited resources.

Europe — The Netherlands

## 122 SCHRÖDER HOUSE (1924)

By Gerrit Rietveld
Prins Hendriklaan 50, 3583 EP Utrecht, The Netherlands

**TO VISIT BEFORE YOU DIE BECAUSE**

Step inside a three-dimensional Mondrian painting, one of the best-known examples of De Stijl architecture.

The Schröder home by Gerrit Rietveld (1888–1964) is the most impressive architectural statement of De Stijl, the avant-garde movement that Rietveld joined in 1918. The architect and furniture designer was commissioned to design the home of Truus Schröder, a wealthy Utrecht widow with whom he started a relationship. With its primary blocks of colour, both inside and out, the house looks like a three-dimensional artwork by Piet Mondrian or Theo van Doesburg, both contemporaries of Rietveld. The design is an exercise in geometry and colour, and although experimental, the house is a practical, liveable home. Architecture-lovers visiting the house are issued with plastic overshoes so as not to damage the interior. Rietveld's extraordinary solutions for the living areas express a furniture designer's eye for detail. He came up with clever ideas such as sliding walls to create a flexible layout – rooms could be bigger or smaller depending on their function or the time of day. And, in keeping with the geometric principles of De Stijl that favoured right angles, the windows can hinge open to a maximum of 90°. In 1924, when this house was completed, it was hailed as a landmark in innovation. And when you visit the house a hundred or so years later, you'll see that nothing of that radical spirit has been lost.

www.rietveldschroderhuis.nl/nl/rietveld-schroderhuis

Europe     The Netherlands

# 123 JACHTHUIS SINT HUBERTUS (1915)

By Hendrikus Petrus Berlage
Apeldoornseweg 258, 7351 TA Hoenderloo, The Netherlands

**TO VISIT BEFORE YOU DIE BECAUSE**

This house is evidence that Berlage took his obsessive *Gesamtkunstwerk* to such an extreme that he drove his clients to despair.

The famous Kröller-Müller Museum is located in the Hoge Veluwe National Park in the Netherlands, designed by Henry van de Velde for Helene Kröller-Müller's collection. The Jachthuis Sint Hubertus (1915), the former country residence of the Kröller-Müller couple, is less well known. The hunting lodge was not designed by Van de Velde, but by his rival Hendrikus Petrus Berlage (1856-1934). For his design, Berlage drew inspiration from the formal qualities of the archetypal English country house. Yet this project is not an exercise in English style, but an extremely precise *Gesamtkunstwerk* by Berlage. The architect designed everything, including the furniture, the cutlery, the stained-glass windows, and the pond. His uncompromising approach drove the Kröller-Müller couple to despair. What's more, completion was frequently postponed because the artisanal details consumed so much time and money. The construction was finally completed in 1920. For the couple, the pavilion first served as a country retreat, then as a permanent home. In 1935 the building was donated to the Dutch state. It has been open to the public since its restoration.

www.hogeveluwe.nl/nl/ontdek-het-park/kunst-en-architectuur/jachthuis-sint-hubertus

Europe — Norway

## 124 VILLA STENERSEN (1937–1939)

By Arne Korsmo
Tuengen allé 10C, 0374 Oslo, Norway

**TO VISIT BEFORE YOU DIE BECAUSE**

See the Norwegian answer to Le Corbusier's Villa Savoye.

Since undergoing extensive restoration in 2003, Villa Stenersen – one of architecture's hidden gems – has been attracting architecture fans from all over the world every Sunday between May and October. And rightly so: the design by architect Arne Korsmo (1900–1968) is astonishingly light, colourful, and sophisticated. The art collector Rolf E. Stenersen (1899–1978) gave him a substantial budget and carte blanche to design this modern private home. Korsmo's distinctly international style shines out in this functionalist home, which features elements from the Bauhaus as well as from the work of Le Corbusier, Mies van der Rohe, and Alvar Aalto. Notable are the semi-circular drive-through garage (as in Le Corbusier's Villa Savoye), the façade with thick glass bricks (to protect the art collection), the 625 glass cylinders in shades of blue, and the soft colours (as in Aalto's Paimio Sanatorium). Stenersen donated the house to the Norwegian state in 1974, which, among other things, used it as a residence for Prime Minister Odvar Norli. The villa is now part of the National Museum of Art.

Europe     Poland

# 125   KERET HOUSE (2012)

By Jakub Szczęsny
Żelazna 74, 00-875 Warsaw, Poland

TO VISIT
BEFORE YOU DIE
BECAUSE

**Measuring 92 centimetres at its narrowest point, this is the world's skinniest house.**

Technically, Keret House is not a home, but an art installation: according to Warsaw housing regulations, it is too small to be classified as a house. But architect Jakub Szczęsny (born 1973) designed the ultra-narrow house for a patron, the Israeli filmmaker and writer Etgar Keret. For Keret, the skinny house also holds symbolic meaning: he considers it a 'memorial' to his family who were killed when the Nazis invaded Poland. If you're claustrophobic, this may not be the house for you: at its narrowest point, it measures 92 centimetres, and is 152 centimetres at its widest. And yet there is room for a living area, bedroom, bathroom, and lounge. You must climb a folding ladder to reach the second floor of this wafer-thin house, inserted into the space between a brick building and a concrete apartment block. Architect Jakub Szczęsny also sees his installation as an indictment of the inconsistent building policy of the city of Warsaw, which creates unsightly voids between structures. Visitors must make a booking to visit the house.

www.kerethouse.com/

Europe — Poland

# 126 OSKAR HANSEN HOUSE (1969–1970)

By Oskar Hansen
Ul. Mlekicie 4, 07-130 Szumin, Poland

**TO VISIT BEFORE YOU DIE BECAUSE**

Located in a picturesque area of an oxbow lake of the River Bug, this house is perpetually evolving, its users participating in its creation.

Some people refer to this house in Szumin, Poland, as The Sheep Barn. Seeing it from the outside, it's easy to mistake the summer house of Oskar Nikolai Hansen (1922–2005) for random farm architecture. But appearances are deceptive. Once you set foot inside the chalet, the radicality of the design of Oskar and his wife Zofia is clear. Even his children co-designed their summer home in Mazovia, by the River Bug. Hansen was a member of Team 10: a splinter group that arose in 1953 on the fringes of the 9th meeting of the CIAM, an influential international conference for modern architecture and urban planning. At the 1959 CIAM congress, Oskar and Zofia, both architects, rejected the notion of the 'home as a functionalist machine' in favour of their 'open form' theory. The purest realisation of this theory is seen in the house they designed for themselves, between 1969 and 1970, in Szumin. In a sense, its architecture is 'open ended': rather than the architect dictating how the dwelling is used, the Hansen House can be endlessly transformed by its inhabitants. In that sense, the house is constantly in flux, a mutable framework that adapts to the phase of life, character, and individual expression of the inhabitants. For example, Hansen placed a steel structure in the garden, salvaged from the 1977 Venice Biennale, on which he grew grape vines. In 2014, the Museum of Modern Art in Warsaw became custodian of the house. It continues to organise guided tours of this transformable masterpiece, even after its restoration in 2019.

www.artmuseum.pl/pl/wystawy/dom-hansenow-w-szuminie-2

Europe — Portugal

## 127 CASA DAS MARINHAS (1954)

By Alfredo Evangelista Viana de Lima
Rua 24 de Junho, 4740-575 Marinhas, Esposende, Braga, Portugal

**TO VISIT BEFORE YOU DIE BECAUSE**

Portugal's answer to the Eames House, this work of architecture represents a modernist paradise.

Perhaps the best example of Portuguese modernism, which seamlessly blends local and international influences, is 'Casa das Marinhas' in Esposende. Architect Alfredo Evangelista Viana de Lima (1913–1991) designed the house as a personal residence in 1954. Le Corbusier's '5-point plan' is immediately apparent in the exterior, the bands of windows, the colours, and the supporting column. The open plan, playful interior elements and double heights are reminiscent of the Eames House of 1949. In its sensual, organic formal language, the design recalls Oscar Niemeyer, with whom he collaborated on several occasions. But you can also feel the influence of Viana de Lima's tutor, Marques da Silva, celebrated for his Casa Serralves on the outskirts of Porto. Viana de Lima's place in the canon of Portuguese modernism cannot be overstated: he designed some of the country's most important buildings (including the Economics Faculty at the University of Porto). He was also active as an urban planner and as an architecture lecturer in Lisbon and Porto, and he served as a heritage consultant on an extremely varied array of projects that helped put Portuguese architecture on the map.

Europe — Portugal

# 128 VILLA SERRALVES (1931–1944)

By José Marques da Silva and Charles Siclis
Rua de Serralves 97, 4150-708 Porto, Portugal

**TO VISIT BEFORE YOU DIE BECAUSE**

Come for the remarkable pink Portuguese Art Deco mansion; stay for the contemporary art museum and expansive, verdant grounds.

Having recently inherited the family's summer residence, Count Carlos Alberto Cabral – an intellectual industrialist and globetrotter – dreamt of a modern house like the one he had seen at the International Exhibition of Modern Decorative and Industrial Arts in Paris in 1925. He called upon the services of the architect José Marques da Silva (1869–1947), who conceived a new residence in the purest Art Deco style. The property is lit up in a swathe of pink at the top of the park. The arrangement of pools and fountains across the graded terraces reinforces the building's majesty. The interior is just as lavish. It incorporates a panorama of international design from the 1930s and 1940s and is enhanced by the work of renowned artists, including René Lalique, Edgard Brandt, and Jacques Ruhlmann. The villa is part of the Serralves Foundation, which boasts a rich historical and cultural heritage, including the museum designed by the architect Álvaro Siza and the Serralves Park, which was designed by the French architect Jacques Greber.

www.serralves.pt/pt/fundacao/a-casa-de-serralves/

Europe  Russia

# 129 GORKY HOUSE (1900–1903)

By Fyodor Shekhtel
Malaya Nikitskaya Ulitsa 6/2, Moscow, 121069, Russia

**TO VISIT BEFORE YOU DIE BECAUSE**

Step into a world of vibrant details and decadence at the most magnificent Art Nouveau house museum in Moscow.

At the end of the 19th century, Art Nouveau spread from Belgium and France to the rest of Europe. Variants popped up in countries such as Germany, Italy, Austria, Switzerland, the United Kingdom, Finland, Spain, America, and Russia. In Moscow, while a number of Art-Nouveau-style houses are now in use as embassies and are not publicly accessible, the mansion that Fyodor Shekhtel (1859–1926) built between 1900 and 1903 for the businessman S.P. Ryabushinsky is open to visitors. It was the design of this private residence that established the architect's reputation as 'the Gaudí of Russia'. He certainly seemed to share his Catalan contemporary's vivid imagination, with extraordinary carvings and stained-glass windows and mosaics. Inspired by fauna and flora, the interior and exterior are an ode to craftmanship. Visitors to the villa step into a world of vibrant details inspired by seahorses, butterflies, and shells, as well as snails and jellyfish. In his journal, Korney Chukovski, the Russian children's book author, called the house 'the most disgusting piece of decadent style'. Ryabushinsky fled the country in the aftermath of the Russian Revolution in 1917. During the Stalin regime, the house was given to the Russian author Maxim Gorky. Today, the villa is a house museum dedicated to the writer.

www.imli.ru/

Europe — Russia

# 130 MELNIKOV HOUSE (1927–1929)

By Konstantin Melnikov
Krivoarbatsky Ln, 10, Moscow, 119002, Russia

TO VISIT BEFORE YOU DIE BECAUSE

Melnikov's cylindrical house is not to be missed as an important residential constructivist sculpture.

Although Russian Suprematists and constructivists such as Tatlin, Malevich, and El Lissitsky – like their colleagues at De Stijl – had very specific ideas about architecture, few avant-garde residential houses from that revolutionary early 20th century have been preserved in Russia. The Konstantin Melnikov House in Moscow (1927–1929) is an interesting case. The artist's home of architect-painter Melnikov (1890–1974) resembles an experimental constructivist collage composed of two cylinders. One silo is flattened by a huge window, which is rhythmically subdivided. The convex walls of both cylinders are perforated by singular hexagonal windows. The entire building is made up of a honeycomb structure in wood and brick. After the 1917 revolution, Melnikov received various state commissions, including the task of designing the sarcophagus in Lenin's mausoleum in Moscow. In 1925 he delivered the revolutionary pavilion of the Soviet Union for the Exposition Internationale des Arts Décoratifs et Industriels Modernes in Paris. Unwilling to conform to the dictates of Stalinist architectural style, by the mid-1930s Melnikov had largely given up his architectural practice to focus on his art career. His son Victor worked until his death in 2006 to turn the house into a museum that manages the Melnikov archive.

# 131 PLECNIK HOUSE (1921)

By Jože Plečnik
Karunova ulica 4, 1000 Ljubljana, Slovenia

**TO VISIT BEFORE YOU DIE BECAUSE**

Attempt to reconcile the modesty of Slovenia's most famous architect with the grand structures he designed that have left an indelible mark on Ljubljana.

Architecture fans visiting Slovenia have a hard time ignoring Jože Plečnik (1872–1957). He is sometimes referred to as the 'Gaudí of Ljubljana' because of the countless landmark modern buildings he designed: the Triple Bridge, the National Library, the cemetery, and the embankments along the river. At the turn of the 19th century, he also influenced the cityscapes of Prague and Vienna. Jože Plečnik (1872-1957) was originally destined to follow in the footsteps of his father Andrej and take over the family business of carpentry. Fortunately, he opted to become an architect. His career began with Viennese Secession architect Otto Wagner, but in 1911 he moved to Prague, where he renovated Prague Castle. Only when the Ljubljana School of Architecture was founded in 1921 did he return to his native country. That year he bought his own property – a complex with three adjacent houses – where he lived until his death. His former residence is now a house museum. Here, you can learn about his life and work, and discover his collection of stones, his archives, his furniture designs, and his library.

www.mgml.si/sl/plecnikova-hisa/

Europe    Spain

# 132 CAN LIS (1972)

By Jørn Utzon
Ctra. Santanyí-Alqueria Blanca, 81, 07691 Santanyí, Mallorca, Balearic Islands, Spain

TO VISIT
BEFORE YOU DIE
BECAUSE

See the home of the world-famous architect who designed the Sydney Opera House.

Jørn Utzon (1918–2008) is celebrated as the architect of the famous Sydney opera house. But just before that opened – after a challenging 20-year process – he delivered another masterpiece: Can Lis in Mallorca. The Danish architect discovered the Spanish island in the late 1960s when he left Australia. He named the holiday home he designed there after his wife Lis. The house is made up of a series of four pavilions, interconnected by patios, loggias, and terraces. But Can Lis does not feel like four separate structures. The overarching sculptural approach and the sober use of materials evokes a sense of unity: everything is built in local sandstone, sourced from the island. Utzon wanted you to experience the house as if you are looking at the untamed world from within a cave, with landscapes that gradually unfold as you wander through the space. Walking through the house is an almost cinematic experience – every sequence offers a different framing of the surroundings and architecture. The house was in the ownership of the Utzon family until it was acquired by the Utzon Foundation in 2011. Can Lis is now mainly used for working residencies for architects but is also available for rent on a limited basis through the Utzon Foundation. The house only opens to the public on specified Open House days.

www.canlis.dk

Europe — Spain

## 133 CASA BATLLÓ (1904)

By Antoni Gaudí
Passeig de Gracia 43, 08007 Barcelona, Spain

**TO VISIT BEFORE YOU DIE BECAUSE**

Enjoy Gaudí's inspiring imagination in this poetic masterpiece, a hybrid between Jules Verne and Dance Macabre.

For over a century, Antoni Gaudí's landmark designs have defined Barcelona. One of his most original buildings is Casa Battló, also known locally as 'Casa dels Ossos' (literally, the 'House of Bones'). The whimsical private residence of modernismo style draws inspiration from organic skeletal shapes. Commissioned by textile entrepreneur Josep Batlló, Gaudí (1852–1926) converted the existing home into a fabulous 'total work of art' in 1904. Spectacular details are the façade and the atrium, both covered entirely with multicoloured tiles. The house resonates with narrative, artisanal details, both in the ironwork and in the sculpted wood of the railing and doors. When you cross from the 'rib cage' in the attic to the roof terrace, you'll discover the extent of Gaudí's fetish for biomorphic shapes and mosaic: the roof mirrors the arched backbone of a mythical creature. The rooms in Casa Battló are largely unfurnished, but a tablet – which is provided as part of the audio tour – brings the interior virtually to life. The house has been a UNESCO World Heritage Site since 2002, but you are able to enjoy Gaudi's design thanks to the efforts of the current owners.

## 134 CASA MILÀ (1906–1912)

By Antoni Gaudí
Passeig de Gràcia, 92, 08008 Barcelona, Spain

**TO VISIT BEFORE YOU DIE BECAUSE**

Savour the details of this house, including the ornate ironwork, the large light-fused openings, and a stunning roof as surreal as a Dali painting.

Which is the most dazzling residential project designed by Gaudí (1852–1926): Casa Milà or Casa Battló? Both are paragons of the modernismo style of Gaudí's 'mature' period. Just like Battló, Casa Milà has an unusual nickname: 'La Pedrera', or 'The Quarry'. The 7-storey apartment building catches the eye with its undulating stone façade and balconies with ornate ironwork typical of Art Nouveau. As at Casa Battló, Gaudí created large openings in the façade so that sunlight pours into each apartment. The roof is absolutely stunning: the surrealist shapes of the chimneys, skylights, and air vents are like details from a Dali painting. Realised between 1906 and 1912, the building was commissioned by the couple Pere Milà, a property developer, and Roser Segimon, the widow of a wealthy coffee plantation owner. By the end of the 1970s, Gaudí's masterpiece was unrecognisable, having fallen into a state of disrepair. In 1986 Caixa Catalunya bought La Pedrera, and restored it to its former glory. Today, it is part of a UNESCO World Heritage Site and ranks among Barcelona's architectural gems.

www.casabatllo.es   www.lapedrera.com/es

Europe — Spain

# 135 CASA VICENS (1883–1885)

By Antoni Gaudí
Carrer de les Carolines, 20, 08012 Barcelona, Spain

**TO VISIT BEFORE YOU DIE BECAUSE**

The first ever house Gaudí designed, witness what's considered one of the first buildings of Art Nouveau.

If you've already discovered La Pedrera, Casa Battló, and Casa Milá, there's now another reason for you to revisit Barcelona. Casa Vicens is open: the very first house Gaudí (1852–1926) completed. The Spanish architect was only 31 when he was commissioned to build the summer house in the Gracia district for tile producer Manel Vicens i Montaner. It is fascinating to contrast Gaudí's 'modernismo' creations of the early 20th century with his projects from the late 19th century, when his designs were an intoxicating fusion of oriental, Catalan, neoclassical, Gothic, Christian, and Moorish style elements. Casa Vicens, built between 1883 and 1885, is not yet Gaudí at the height of his organic imagination, although the house is a eulogy to his love of craftmanship. In tiles, ceramics, iron, glass, concrete, and papier-mâché, he conjured figurative, graphic, and polychrome details, from which the house derives its uniqueness. The ambitious restoration of Gaudí's 'Manifesto House' – which until then was a residential home – was funded by MoraBanc. After three years of non-stop restoration, it opened to the public as a museum in 2017.

www.casavicens.org

Europe · Spain

# 136 LA FÀBRICA (1975)

By Ricardo Bofill
Av. de la Indústria, 14, 08960 Sant Just Desvern, Barcelona, Spain

TO VISIT BEFORE YOU DIE BECAUSE

Experience a place out of time, located somewhere between Brutalism and Romanticism, where nature seems to have reclaimed its rights.

La Fàbrica perfectly illustrates the concept of architectural regeneration which was so dear to Ricardo Bofill (1939). A veritable cathedral of concrete, it is probably one of the most impressive site renovations ever seen. It was in 1973 that Ricardo Bofill discovered this former disused cement factory near Barcelona, which dates back to the 1920s and is the oldest of its kind in Spain. Then languishing in a state of ruin, it consisted of more than thirty silos equipped with machinery, 4 kilometres of underground galleries, multiple suspended staircases leading nowhere, and unfinished arches. It was an unreal setting, just right for transformation and metamorphosis. The architect decided to preserve the factory and restructure it by sculpting it as a work of art. Some parts were discarded to reveal only the original elements, such as the semi-circular windows, like those found in churches. Other parts were covered or added to – with doors, windows, and façades – providing circulation, space, and perspective. Invaded by plants, the cement factory gave rise to the architect's own home and spaces for exhibitions and concerts. It is also his place of work, where he maintains his office – the Ricardo Bofill Taller de Arquitectura – a group of architects, engineers, sociologists, and philosophers.

Europe — Spain

# 137 LA RICARDA / THE GOMIS HOUSE (1949–1963)

By Antonio Bonet i Castellana
Municipality of El Prat de Llobregat, 08820, Barcelona, Spain

**TO VISIT BEFORE YOU DIE BECAUSE**

Walk along the magnificent roof of this Catalan masterpiece, taking in the stunning views of the surrounding pine forest.

La Ricarda is located in a seaside area near Barcelona, on a plot of land surrounded by a pine forest, near the Mediterranean Sea. It was designed by the Catalan architect Antonio Bonet (1913–1989), in close collaboration with the owners, Ricardo Gomis and Inés Bertrand, two great music-lovers. Very much open to the exterior, this large property stands out for its Catalan vaulted roof, which unifies the whole and forms a harmonious echo to the movement of the surrounding umbrella pines. This harmony is to be found in even the smallest details of construction and decoration, such as the doors, the furniture, and the carpets, as well as in the combination of colours. Walls employing coloured glass in brick claustra give a luminous, transparent effect that gently breaks the boundary between the interior and the exterior. During the Franco dictatorship, *La Ricarda* became a place for all kinds of artistic creation and experimentation. It also served as a refuge for artists and intellectuals such as John Cage, Merce Cunningham, and Joan Miró.

www.elprat.cat/turisme-i-territori/que-visitar/la-casa-gomis

Europe — Spain

# 138 SOLO HOUSE (2017)

By OFFICE Kersten Geers David Van Severen
44623 Cretas, Teruel, Spain

**TO VISIT BEFORE YOU DIE BECAUSE**

This circular house delivers a breathtaking experience of the landscape.

Mattaraña, a remote part of northeast Spain, is home to the Solo House project. It was here, in a location a little over two hours from Barcelona, amongst the inhospitable nature of Aragon and Catalonia, that a French entrepreneur conceived the ambitious plan in 2010 to create a site where avant-garde architects were given carte blanche to design a conceptual dream home. Two Solo Houses have already been completed: a stairway-accessed concrete sculpture by Pezo and Von Ellrichshausen and a circular home by the Belgian architecture studio OFFICE Kersten Geers David Van Severen. The Solo House project is related to the Case Study Houses: an architectural experiment of the *Arts & Architecture* magazine that ran from 1945 to 1966. You can rent the Solo House by OFFICE Kersten Geers David Van Severen. Spending a weekend there is a unique experience: sliding façade sections can be fully or partially drawn aside to open up the living areas to the surrounding landscape or swimming pool. The technical volumes on the roof are indeed functional, but were painted by the artist Pieter Vermeersch, a friend of the architects.

www.solo-houses.com

Europe — Spain

# 139 VOLCANO HOUSE (1968)

By César Manrique
El Taro de Tahíche, Calle Jorge Luis Borges, 16, 35507, Tahíche, Lanzarote, Canary Islands, Spain

**TO VISIT BEFORE YOU DIE BECAUSE**

In a building which engages in constant dialogue with its natural surrounds, enjoy a taste of life inside a volcano.

César Manrique (1919–1992) fell in love with his native island of Lanzarote in the Canary Islands. His architecture is an ode to nature and his intervention in the natural space is very particular. A cultural centre, a garden with more than 1000 species of cacti, a restaurant, a belvedere, and a hotel: all of Manrique's projects are in close dialogue with their natural environment, in a relationship of deep respect. He built his own house in the middle of a frozen lava flow, produced by the great volcanic eruptions that the island experienced between 1730 and 1736. The house extends over 1800 m², with 1200 m² of terraces and gardens over an estate of 3 hectares. It was his home for 20 years, from 1968 to 1988. With its cubic volumes, the upper floor is inspired by the traditional architecture of Lanzarote, to which Manrique added modern elements: large glass windows, magnificent views, and generous spaces. The lower floor is built from the starting point of five natural volcanic bubbles, which have been turned into rooms in which to live: with a lounge, a dance floor, and relaxation areas. They are connected by whitewashed tunnels, one of which has a palm tree growing out of it. In addition to the relaxing atmosphere of the house, the colours are richly contrasted: the brilliant white of the walls with the black of the basalt, the blue of the lagoon-style swimming pool, and the green of the tropical vegetation. This is an incredible house that marries the organic with the inorganic, in a style worthy of a James Bond landmark. It has been the headquarters of the César Manrique Foundation since 1982.

www.fcmanrique.org/

Europe  Switzerland

# 140 HAUS DULDECK (1913–1915)

By Rudolf Steiner
Rüttiweg 15, 4143 Dornach, Switzerland

**TO VISIT BEFORE YOU DIE BECAUSE**

Ponder over the twisted surfaces and curves of this anthroposophical house, designed by the founder of the Steiner philosophy.

The Goetheanum in Dornach, near Basel, is the world's finest example of anthroposophical architecture. Designed by the Austrian pedagogue-architect-philosopher Rudolf Steiner (1861–1925), the concrete building is exceptional for its strikingly organic forms. Several other fascinating examples of anthroposophical-style residential architecture can be found in the vicinity of the 'expressionist' Goetheanum. You can visit one of them, Haus Duldeck, by making an advance reservation. The building was also Steiner's first residential project: a home for dentist Emil Grosheintz and his family. Steiner designed the house as a thank-you for the large plot of land the family donated, and on which the founder of anthroposophy could build his first Goetheanum. Designed and built between 1913 and 1915, the house is one of the most ground-breaking concrete houses of the early 20th century. Steiner worked closely with architect Hermann Ranzenberger on the project, and said: 'It is important that such a house is built someday. Then it stands there as a living protest against everything related to traditional construction.'

www.rudolf-steiner.com/uber-uns/haus-duldeck/

Europe · Switzerland

# 141 MAISON BLANCHE (1912)

By Le Corbusier
Chemin de Pouillerel 12, 2300 La Chaux-de-Fonds, Switzerland

**TO VISIT BEFORE YOU DIE BECAUSE**

Experience the very first residence that Le Corbusier designed.

La Maison Blanche (1912) occupies a special place in the oeuvre of Le Corbusier, known at that time simply as Charles-Édouard Jeanneret (1887-1965). The residence he designed for his parents in his birthplace La-Chaux-de-Fonds is his most important early work. He clearly distances himself from the regional style of architecture in Switzerland. The reason for this is that, in previous years, Jeanneret had gained vital experience in the studios of Auguste Perret (Paris) and Peter Behrens (where Mies van der Rohe and Walter Gropius also worked). The Maison Blanche was his biggest assignment to date, and he immediately seized the opportunity to experiment with new formal principles. The entire home is structured around four pillars, which allow all the remaining interior walls to be removed or repositioned freely. He also housed his newly established office in a room at the Maison Blanche. It is striking how his sober office space differs from the rest of the richly decorated home. In 1919, Le Corbusier's parents sold the villa, and successive owners mutilated its design. But after intensive restoration, the house is classified as a UNESCO World Heritage Site and is open to the public.

www.maisonblanche.ch

Europe — Switzerland

## 142 VILLA "LE LAC" (1923)

By Le Corbusier
Route de Lavaux 21, 1802 Corseaux, Switzerland

**TO VISIT BEFORE YOU DIE BECAUSE**

This villa, designated Swiss Cultural Property of National Significance and added to the UNESCO World Heritage List in 2016, heralds the accomplishments that would lie ahead for Le Corbusier.

Built facing Lake Geneva, this small 'machine for living' was completed in the same year that its designer Le Corbusier published his book *Towards a New Architecture*. The Villa constitutes a typological standard for the research on minimal housing that he would maintain throughout his life. A true feat of engineering, it was created for his parents (his mother lived in it until the time of her death at the age of 100) and it prefigures the villas he was to produce later in his career. Of modest dimensions, it is a rectangular, single-storey parallelepiped measuring 64 m$^2$, featuring a single window 11 metres in length and only 4 metres away from the lake. This window is probably the most important part of the house, transforming it into an observatory that looks out onto both the lake and the Grammont and extending the view on the outside of the house. Le Corbusier added a garden enclosed by three walls, and incorporated a square window that imposes a frame on the landscape which circumscribes our gaze.

www.villalelac.ch

Europe — United Kingdom

# 143 BARBICAN ESTATE (1965–1976)

By Chamberlin, Powell & Bon
Barbican, London, England, EC2Y 8BN, United Kingdom

**TO VISIT BEFORE YOU DIE BECAUSE**

Get two for one at the Barbican: a classic of Brutalism and a trip to the magnificent Arts Centre.

The origin of the name comes from the French *barbacane* – a medieval rampart. This high-end residential complex is in fact built on the remains of the walls of the Roman city of Londinium, and one can still see a remnant of the Roman rampart on the site. The Barbican was born out of a need to create new housing in post-war London for the city's wealthy professionals and their families. A veritable temple to Brutalism, the site consists of 2000 apartments, houses, and maisonettes, all connected by a concrete walkway above street level, and offering a pedestrian route amidst the ponds, fountains, and gardens. The dwellings contain all the latest technical advances of the time, including showers. The Barbican estate was soon followed by the construction of the exceptional cultural centre of the same name, which was inaugurated in 1982.

www.barbican.org.uk/whats-on/series/barbican-tours

Europe — United Kingdom

# 144 BLACKWELL (1901)

By Mackay Hugh Baillie Scott
Bowness-on-Windermere, Cumbria, England, LA23 3JT, United Kingdom

**TO VISIT BEFORE YOU DIE BECAUSE**

Standing at the crossroads between Victorian and Modern architecture, this house is the most sumptuous of the Arts and Crafts style homes in the Lake District.

Around the turn of the 19th century, Sir Edward Holt, a wealthy brewer from Manchester, challenged architect Mackay Hugh Baillie Scott (1865–1945) to design a holiday home in the Lake District as an all-embracing Arts and Crafts style work of art. Holt came to live in Blackwell in 1901 with his wife and five children. As if the spectacular view of Lake Windermere isn't enough, the traditional interior finish in timber, tile, stained glass, decorative plaster, and wallpaper will leave you breathless. There are so many gorgeous details to discover as you roam this ravishingly restored property – features often inspired by flora and fauna, the embodiment of the Arts and Crafts movement. Although the architect was evidently influenced by medieval architecture, this house was equipped with the latest amenities, including electric light and central heating. Blackwell has a restless history: after the Holts, the house became a school, and later an office space. But after being purchased by Lakeland Arts, the Lake District's most exceptional Arts and Crafts house was fully restored and opened to the public in 2001.

www.blackwell.org.uk

Europe — United Kingdom

# 145 CHARLESTON HOUSE (1916–1978)

By Bloomsbury Group
Firle, West Firle, Lewes, England, BN8 6LL, United Kingdom

**TO VISIT BEFORE YOU DIE BECAUSE**

Pay homage to the birthplace of the experimental and sincere DIY philosophy adopted by a famous artists' commune.

Vanessa Bell, Virginia Woolf, Maynard Keynes, Duncan Grant: with their bohemian lifestyles, the artists and thinkers of the Bloomsbury Group were an LGTBQ collective that practised co-housing, upcycling, and free love. The group members got to know each other during their student days at Cambridge and began to meet in a house in Bloomsbury, London, in 1905. When Virginia Woolfe told them about Charleston House in Sussex, in the south of England, it became a focal point for the group. The house was fairly primitive, but that didn't stop the artists, who took over the place completely. Immediately, they began painting everything in the house, from bedsteads to tables, from chairs to library cabinets, creating a unique DIY interior. In their Omega Workshops, the group members also painted and made ceramics, furniture, clothing, crockery, and carpets. The artists who stayed here didn't follow hard and fast rules about what good architecture or interior design should be. They were free to experiment, and shaped a vibrant artists' colony, forever fluid and hugely inspiring.

www.charleston.org.uk

Europe — United Kingdom

# 146 ELTHAM PALACE (1936)

By John Seely and Paul Edward Paget
Court Yard, London, England, SE9 5QE, United Kingdom

**TO VISIT BEFORE YOU DIE BECAUSE**

Relive a glamour reminiscent of *The Great Gatsby*, or behold the grandour of Netflix's *The Crown*.

If you dream of visiting a home that radiates the glitz and glamour of the interbellum years, Eltham Palace in Greenwich, London, is a must-see. The architects John Seely (1899 - 1963) and Paul Edward Paget (1901 - 1985) were given creative carte blanche for the opulent residence of Sir Stephen and Virginia Courtauld, a high-society couple who were both fashionable and aristocratic. The history of the palace – which had served as a royal residence for centuries – can be traced back to 1305. The most striking feature is the interiors, among the most sumptuous of the Art Deco period. The house is not a *Gesamtkunstwerk* by Seely and Paget; the architects collaborated with a number of designers, including Rolf Engströmer, to realise the spectacular entrance hall with its iconic domed glass ceiling. The classicist-inspired dining room, bathroom, and bedroom were designed by the Italian interior designer and socialite Piero Malacrida, who previously worked for Stephen Courtauld's brother Samuel - the founder of the famous Courtauld Institute of Art. It is quite possible that the interior of Eltham Palace will ring a bell: this is where season 2 of *The Crown* was filmed.

www.english-heritage.org.uk/visit/places/eltham-palace-and-gardens

Europe United Kingdom

# 147 THE HILL HOUSE (1902–1904)

By Charles Rennie Mackintosh
Upper Colquhoun St, Helensburgh, Scotland, G84 9AJ, United Kingdom

**TO VISIT BEFORE YOU DIE BECAUSE**

Be inspired by the unique building, interiors, and collection designed by Mackintosh in the 'Glasgow style'.

Situated on the top of a hill overlooking the River Clyde, the house combines neo-Gothic and Arts and Crafts styles. It also features the large, clean, pared-back volumes so dear to the architect's heart. The white room specially designed for the client – the publisher Walter Blackie – is one of the most famous rooms that Mackintosh (1868 - 1928) produced. This is the room for which he created the emblematic Hill House chair, the eponymous model made for the house. Its astonishing dimensions, 141 cm high and 41 cm wide, make it a unique example in the history of design. The blackness of the chair cuts a stark contrast with the whiteness of the room, and its chequered backrest evokes Mackintosh's taste for the square, contrasting with the stylised flowers of the wallpaper.

# 148 BOYD II RESIDENCE (1958)

By Robin Boyd
290 Walsh Street, South Yarra, 3141 Victoria, Australia

**TO VISIT BEFORE YOU DIE BECAUSE**

Robin Boyd's 1958 masterpiece, a time machine of architecture, exemplifies the importance he attached to design that responds to the Australian climate, lifestyle, and character.

Together with Rose Seidler House of 1950 (p.250), Robin Boyd's private residence, built in 1958, is a paradigm of modernist Australian architecture. The house is widely regarded as Boyd's masterpiece and the purest embodiment of his visionary view of residential architecture. As the author of the polemical book *The Australian Ugliness* (1960), Robin Boyd (1919–1971) argued for a national style of architecture, rooted in Australian identity. His house on Walsh Street is an audacious start. The dwelling consists of two wings – each with a sloping roof line – both of which open onto a green courtyard that simultaneously provides intimacy and light. Thanks to a clever split-level structure, Boyd created a tightly organised interior space, more compact than that of the average suburban home: a form of space wastage that he fulminated against. Since 2006, the house has been home to the Robin Boyd Foundation, which conducts research, organises seminars, and gives guided tours. As the foundation bought the house directly from Boyd's widow Patricia Davies, the design is still completely authentic. Even Boyd's library, art collection, and furniture, created by luminaries such as Grant Featherston and Clement Meadmore, are still intact.

# 149 BUTTERFLY HOUSE (1955)

By Peter McIntyre
2 Hodgson Street, Kew, 3101 Victoria, Australia

**TO VISIT BEFORE YOU DIE BECAUSE**

This joyous, colourful house embodies McIntyre's striking style as well as the post-war Melbourne regional style.

The architect Peter McIntyre (1927) built his house on a very steep piece of land, which imposed constraints on the overall design. The entrance to the house is via a series of rough-cut sandstone steps that contrast with the geometric rigour of the façade. The dark wooden panels were originally made of red-and-yellow painted Stramit (a material made of compressed straw), but these were replaced in the 1960s. In the interior, the bright, bold colours evoke a Russian constructivist painting. The spiral staircase and triangular windows create the dynamic lines so typical of the Australian architect in the middle of the 1950s.

www.sydneylivingmuseums.com.au/stories/butterfly-house

Oceania — Australia

# 150 ROSE SEIDLER HOUSE (1950)

By Harry Seidler
69–71 Clissold Road, Wahroonga, New South Wales 2076, Australia

**TO VISIT BEFORE YOU DIE BECAUSE**

This is the most influential Modernist home in Australia.

The fact that the Australian architect Harry Seidler (1923–2006) was taught at Harvard by Walter Gropius and worked for two years in Marcel Breuer's office is no surprise when you study his Rose Seidler House. He built the mid-century masterpiece in 1948–1950 for his parents, Rose and Max Seidler. Because Rose was so closely involved with the architectural project, the heritage-listed house is usually named only after her. The Corbusian stilt house is a white box that is connected to the garden via a large walkway and a garden wall. Due to its modernity and spatial concept, the house broke with the conventions of post-war Australian architecture. Not surprisingly, the 'Villa Savoye of Sydney' was sometimes called the most influential home in the country. For Seidler, too, it kickstarted a career in his native country: in more than fifty years he built private homes, office buildings, and apartment blocks.

# Index 150 Houses

| | | |
|---|---|---|
| Aalto House . . . . . . . . . . . . . . . . . . . . .137 | Gropius House . . . . . . . . . . . . . . . . . . . .70 | Saarinen House . . . . . . . . . . . . . . . . . 96 |
| Alan I W Frank House . . . . . . . . . . . .50 | Habitat 67 . . . . . . . . . . . . . . . . . . . . . . . .35 | Schindler House. . . . . . . . . . . . . . . . . .95 |
| Alden B. Dow Home and Studio . . . . .51 | Harvey House. . . . . . . . . . . . . . . . . . . . .87 | Schminke House . . . . . . . . . . . . . . . 189 |
| Barbican Estate . . . . . . . . . . . . . . . . . 240 | Haus am Horn . . . . . . . . . . . . . . . . . .178 | Schröder House . . . . . . . . . . . . . . . . .215 |
| Bawa House . . . . . . . . . . . . . . . . . . . . .110 | Haus Duldeck. . . . . . . . . . . . . . . . . . .237 | Schwartz House, The . . . . . . . . . . . . . 82 |
| Blackwell. . . . . . . . . . . . . . . . . . . . . . . .241 | Haus Hohe Pappeln . . . . . . . . . . . . . 180 | Sheats-Goldstein House, The . . . . . . 90 |
| Boyd II Residence . . . . . . . . . . . . . . .247 | Haus Lange und Haus Esters . . . . . 182 | Solo House . . . . . . . . . . . . . . . . . . . . 235 |
| Brummel House. . . . . . . . . . . . . . . . .132 | Haus Ungers. . . . . . . . . . . . . . . . . . . . 183 | Sonneveld House. . . . . . . . . . . . . . . .210 |
| Butterfly House . . . . . . . . . . . . . . . . . 246 | Hill House, The . . . . . . . . . . . . . . . . 244 | Stahl House . . . . . . . . . . . . . . . . . . . . 99 |
| Cabanon, Le . . . . . . . . . . . . . . . . . . . .143 | Hirsch Apartment, The . . . . . . . . . .134 | Studio-Apartment |
| Can Lis. . . . . . . . . . . . . . . . . . . . . . . . .227 | Hohenhof . . . . . . . . . . . . . . . . . . . . . .181 | of Le Corbusier . . . . . . . . . . . . . . . . 162 |
| Casa Aberta . . . . . . . . . . . . . . . . . . . . .19 | Hollyhock House. . . . . . . . . . . . . . . . .72 | Studio-Home |
| Casa Azul . . . . . . . . . . . . . . . . . . . . . . .39 | Horta Museum. . . . . . . . . . . . . . . . . .118 | of Theo van Doesburg . . . . . . . . . . 166 |
| Casa Barragán . . . . . . . . . . . . . . . . . . .38 | Hôtel Martel. . . . . . . . . . . . . . . . . . . .145 | Taliesin East. . . . . . . . . . . . . . . . . . . .101 |
| Casa Battló . . . . . . . . . . . . . . . . . . . . 228 | Hôtel Max Hallet. . . . . . . . . . . . . . . .117 | Taut's Haus . . . . . . . . . . . . . . . . . . . 193 |
| Casa Crespi . . . . . . . . . . . . . . . . . . . . 194 | Hôtel Otlet . . . . . . . . . . . . . . . . . . . . .121 | Tyler Residence . . . . . . . . . . . . . . . . . 98 |
| Casa das Canoas. . . . . . . . . . . . . . . . .18 | Hôtel Solvay . . . . . . . . . . . . . . . . . . . .120 | Umbrella House. . . . . . . . . . . . . . . . .104 |
| Casa das Marinhas . . . . . . . . . . . . . . 222 | Hvitträsk. . . . . . . . . . . . . . . . . . . . . . .140 | van Schijndel House. . . . . . . . . . . . . .213 |
| Casa de Vidro . . . . . . . . . . . . . . . . . . 26 | Jachthuis Sint Hubertus . . . . . . . . . 216 | Villa "Le Lac" . . . . . . . . . . . . . . . . . . . 239 |
| Casa Estudio Diego Rivera . . . . . . . . . . | James Rose Center . . . . . . . . . . . . . . .74 | Villa Beer. . . . . . . . . . . . . . . . . . . . . . .116 |
| y Frida Kahlo . . . . . . . . . . . . . . . . . . .41 | Jan de Jong House . . . . . . . . . . . . . . 206 | Villa Borsani. . . . . . . . . . . . . . . . . . . . 198 |
| Casa Milà. . . . . . . . . . . . . . . . . . . . . . 228 | Jeanneret House . . . . . . . . . . . . . . . . 108 | Villa Cavrois . . . . . . . . . . . . . . . . . . . 168 |
| Casa Modernista . . . . . . . . . . . . . . . . .32 | Judd Foundation . . . . . . . . . . . . . . . . .52 | Villa E-1027 . . . . . . . . . . . . . . . . . . . .170 |
| Casa O'Gorman . . . . . . . . . . . . . . . . .43 | Kentuck Knob. . . . . . . . . . . . . . . . . . .75 | Villa Empain. . . . . . . . . . . . . . . . . . . .123 |
| Casa Orgánica . . . . . . . . . . . . . . . . . 46 | Keret House . . . . . . . . . . . . . . . . . . . 218 | Villa Falbala . . . . . . . . . . . . . . . . . . . .171 |
| Casa Oscar Americano. . . . . . . . . . . .23 | Kiefhoek Residence. . . . . . . . . . . . . .214 | Villa Leoni. . . . . . . . . . . . . . . . . . . . . 200 |
| Casa Remo Brindisi. . . . . . . . . . . . . .195 | Korman House. . . . . . . . . . . . . . . . . . .78 | Villa Mairea . . . . . . . . . . . . . . . . . . . .141 |
| Casa Saldarini . . . . . . . . . . . . . . . . . .197 | Liljestrand House . . . . . . . . . . . . . . . 80 | Villa Majorelle (France) . . . . . . . . . .172 |
| Casa Vicens. . . . . . . . . . . . . . . . . . . . 230 | Louis Carré House. . . . . . . . . . . . . . .146 | Villa Müller. . . . . . . . . . . . . . . . . . . . .134 |
| Casa Vilanova Artigas . . . . . . . . . . . . .22 | Lunuganga . . . . . . . . . . . . . . . . . . . . .111 | Villa Necchi-Campiglio . . . . . . . . . . 199 |
| Casa Walther Moreira Salles . . . . . . . .31 | Maison Berteaux . . . . . . . . . . . . . . . . 126 | Villa Noailles . . . . . . . . . . . . . . . . . . .175 |
| Charleston House . . . . . . . . . . . . . . . 242 | Maison Blanche. . . . . . . . . . . . . . . . . 238 | Villa Oasis (Morocco) . . . . . . . . . . . . .11 |
| De Beir House. . . . . . . . . . . . . . . . . .129 | Maison Unal. . . . . . . . . . . . . . . . . . . .153 | Villa on the Rocks . . . . . . . . . . . . . . .174 |
| Diagoon Housing. . . . . . . . . . . . . . . 204 | Maisons La Roche-Jeanneret . . . . . .150 | Villa Ottolenghi . . . . . . . . . . . . . . . . 202 |
| Domenig Steinhaus. . . . . . . . . . . . . .112 | Manitoga. . . . . . . . . . . . . . . . . . . . . . .81 | Villa Planchart . . . . . . . . . . . . . . . . . 106 |
| Eames House . . . . . . . . . . . . . . . . . . . .53 | Masters' Houses . . . . . . . . . . . . . . . . 186 | Villa Ronde . . . . . . . . . . . . . . . . . . . . .14 |
| Elrod House . . . . . . . . . . . . . . . . . . . .54 | Melnikov House. . . . . . . . . . . . . . . . 225 | Villa Savoye. . . . . . . . . . . . . . . . . . . . .176 |
| Eltham Palace . . . . . . . . . . . . . . . . . 243 | Miller House. . . . . . . . . . . . . . . . . . . . 84 | Villa Serralves . . . . . . . . . . . . . . . . . 223 |
| Fàbrica, La . . . . . . . . . . . . . . . . . . . . .231 | Modulightor Building, The . . . . . . . . 86 | Villa Stenersen. . . . . . . . . . . . . . . . . .217 |
| Fallingwater House. . . . . . . . . . . . . . .55 | Muuratsalo Experimental House. . .142 | Villa Stuck. . . . . . . . . . . . . . . . . . . . . 184 |
| Farnsworth House. . . . . . . . . . . . . . . .58 | Neutra VDL House . . . . . . . . . . . . . . 88 | Villa Winternitz. . . . . . . . . . . . . . . . .133 |
| Finn Juhl's House . . . . . . . . . . . . . . .136 | Oskar Hansen House . . . . . . . . . . . . 220 | Villa Zevaco . . . . . . . . . . . . . . . . . . . .16 |
| Frank Lloyd Wright House . . . . . . . . .59 | Palacio de Abraxas . . . . . . . . . . . . . .156 | Volcano House . . . . . . . . . . . . . . . . . 236 |
| Frank Sinatra House. . . . . . . . . . . . . . 60 | Palmer House. . . . . . . . . . . . . . . . . . . 89 | Wall House #2 . . . . . . . . . . . . . . . . .207 |
| Frederick C. Robie House. . . . . . . . . .61 | Plecnik House . . . . . . . . . . . . . . . . . 226 | Weissenhofsiedlung . . . . . . . . . . . . . 192 |
| Frey House II . . . . . . . . . . . . . . . . . . . 62 | Postman Cheval's Ideal Palace . . . . .158 | Weizmann House . . . . . . . . . . . . . . . 109 |
| Futuro House . . . . . . . . . . . . . . . . . .139 | Prairie House . . . . . . . . . . . . . . . . . . . 94 | Wichita House . . . . . . . . . . . . . . . . . . .97 |
| Gamble House . . . . . . . . . . . . . . . . . . 62 | Private residence of Jean Prouvé. . 160 | |
| Garcia House . . . . . . . . . . . . . . . . . . .65 | Radiant City Housing Unit, The. . . .161 | |
| Ghost Ranch. . . . . . . . . . . . . . . . . . . .65 | Renaat Braem Huis . . . . . . . . . . . . . .130 | |
| Glass House, The . . . . . . . . . . . . . . . 66 | Résidence Le Point du Jour . . . . . . . .159 | |
| Gorky House. . . . . . . . . . . . . . . . . . 224 | Ricarda, La . . . . . . . . . . . . . . . . . . . . 234 | |
| Grace Miller House . . . . . . . . . . . . . . 66 | Rose Seidler House . . . . . . . . . . . . . . 250 | |

© Photos

pp. 10 – 11 © Luc Viatour / pp. 12 – 13 © Nicolas Matheus / pp. 14 – 15 © Stefano Berca / pp. 16 – 17 © Jacinthe Gigou / p. 18 © Niemeyer, Oscar – SABAM Belgium, 2021 - © Michel Moch / p. 19 © Leonardo Finotti / pp. 20 – 21 © Nelson Kon / p. 22 © Instituto Casa Vilanova Artigas / p. 23 © Nelson Kon / pp. 24 – 25 © Renato Leary / pp. 27 – 29 © Leonardo Finotti / pp. 30 – 31 © Robert Polidori photograph IMS / pp. 32 – 33 Pedro Kok / p. 34 © Safdie Architects / pp. 36 – 37 © Timothy Hursley / p. 38 © Barragán Foundation, Switzerland – SABAM Belgium pour les oeuvres de Barragán et leurs photographies par Salas Portugal © Barragán Foundation / p. 39 © Image Select / p. 40 © 2021 Banco de México Diego Rivera Frida Kahlo Museums Trust, Mexico, D.F. – SABAM Belgium - © Leonardo Finotti / pp. 42 – 45 © SABAM Belgium 2021 - © Lorenzo Zandri / pp. 46 – 49 © Javier Senosiain / p. 50 © SABAM Belgium 2021 - © Alan I W Frank House Foundation / p. 51 The Alden B. Dow Home and Studio courtesy of the Alden B. Dow Archives, photography by Balthazar Korab / p. 52 © Judd Foundation – SABAM Belgium 2021 - Photo Matthew Millman © Judd Foundation / p. 53 © Eames Office LLC (eamesoffice.com), photo by Leslie Schwartz / p. 54 © Juergen Nogai, © John Lautner Foundation / p. 55 – 57 © SABAM Belgium 2021 - © Andrew Pielage, courtesy of the Western Pennsylvania Conservancy / p. 58 © SABAM Belgium 2021 - © Image Select / p. 59 © SABAM Belgium - © Image Select / p. 60 © Image Select / p. 61 © SABAM Belgium 2021 © Image Select / p. 63 top © Richard Powers / p. 63 bottom © Alexander Vertikoff - Vertikoff Archive / p. 64 top © Raymond Meier, © John Lautner Foundation / p. 64 bottom © Georgia O'Keeffe Museum – SABAM Belgium, 2021 – Photo Herbert Lotz © Georgia O'Keeffe Museum / p. 67 top © Tara Wujcik, with the help of the Neutra Institute for Survival Through Design / p. 67 bottom – 69 © Eirik Johnson courtesy the Glass House (theglasshouse.org) / pp. 70 – 71 © SABAM Belgium 2021 - Courtesy of Historic New England / pp. 72 – 73 © SABAM Belgium 2021 - © Andrew Pielage / p. 74 © Image Select / pp. 75 – 77 © SABAM Belgium 2021 - © Andrew Pielage / pp. 78 – 79 © Matt Wargo / p. 80 © Bob Liljestrand / p. 81 © Manitoga / The Russel Wright Design Center, photography Vivian Linares / pp. 82 – 83 © SABAM Belgium 2021 - © Andrew Pielage / pp. 84 – 85 Photo courtesy Newfields / p. 86 © Image Select / p. 87 © Romi Cortier / p. 88 © J. Paul Getty Trust. Getty Research Institute, Los Angeles (2004.R.10) / p. 89 © SABAM Belgium 2021 with permission from FLW Palmer House LLC / p. 90 © 2018 Mark Hertzberg / pp. 90 – 93 © Tom Ferguson, © John Lautner Foundation / p. 94 Herb Greene, Prairie House, 1961. Robert A. Bowlby Collection, American School Archives, University of Oklahoma Libraries / p. 95 © Joshua White / p. 96 © Richard Powers / p. 97 Image of the Collections of the Henry Ford / p. 99 top © Romi Cortier / p. 99 bottom © Romi Cortier / p. 100 & pp. 102 – 103 © SABAM Belgium 2021 - © Andrew Pielage / pp. 104 – 105 © Anton Grassl / p. 106 – 107 © Antoine Baralhe / p. 108 © SABAM Belgium 2021 - © Paul Clemence / p. 109 © Mikaela Burstow / p. 110 © Lunuganga Trust / p. 111 © Lunuganga Trust / pp. 112 – 115 © Gerhard Maurer / p. 116 © www.studiohuger.at / p. 117 © Sophie Voituron / pp. 118 – 119 © Paul Louis / p. 120 © Sophie Voituron / p. 121 © SABAM Belgium 2021 - © Image Select / pp. 122 – 123 Boghossian Foundation – Villa Empain © Georges De Kinder / pp. 124 – 125 © Jacinthe Gigou / pp. 126 – 127 © Jan Verlinde / p. 128 © Jeroen Verrecht / p. 129 © Thijs Demeulemeester / p. 130 © Jacinthe Gigou / p. 131 © Oswald Pauwels / p. 132 © Image Select / p. 133 © David Cysař / p. 135 top © Adolf Loos Apartment and Gallery Prague / p. 135 bottom © The City of Prague Museum, photography by Martin Polák / p. 136 © One Collection, photography by Realdania By & Byg Klubben / p. 137 The Aalto House, Helsinki. Alvar Aalto 1935-36. Living room. Photo: Maija Holma, Alvar Aalto Foundation. 2018 / pp. 138 – 139 © Craig Barnes / p. 140 © Mikko Teräsvirta / p. 141 © Mairea Foundation, photography by Rauno Träskelin / p. 142 Muuratsalo Experimental House, Jyväskylä. Alvar Aalto 1952-54. View to the south, to the patio. Photo: Maija Holma, Alvar Aalto Foundation. 2018 / p. 143 © F.L.C. - SABAM Belgium 2021, Olivier Martin Gambier / pp. 144 – 145 © Jacinthe Gigou / p. 146 © Kaminoto.com – Secundino Hernandez / p. 147 © Kaminoto.com / pp. 148 – 149 © Lucie Jean – Kees Visser / pp. 150 – 151 © F.L.C. - SABAM Belgium 2021 - © Image Select / pp. 152 – 155 © Claude Unal, photography: Joël Unal / pp. 156-157 © RBTA / p. 158 © Collection Palais idéal - Frédéric Jouhanin / p. 159 © Sophie Masse / p. 160 © SABAM Belgium 2021 - © Manuel Bougot / p. 161 © F.L.C. - SABAM Belgium 2021, photography: Jacinthe Gigou / pp. 162 – 165 © F.L.C. - SABAM Belgium 2021, photography: Olivier Martin Gambier / pp. 166 – 167 © Jean-Michel Bale / pp. 168 – 169 © Jacinthe Gigou / p. 170 © Manuel Bougot / p. 171 © SABAM Belgium 2021 - © Fondation Dubuffet / pp. 172 – 173 © SABAM Belgium 2021 - © MEN - Cliché Siméon Levaillant, 2019 / p. 175 top © Image Select / p. 175 bottom Clos Saint-Bernard, known as villa Noailles, Hyères art center of national interest Métropole Toulon Provence Méditerranée © photographer Richard Powers / p. 176 © F.L.C. - SABAM Belgium 2021, photography: Jacinthe Gigou / p. 177 © F.L.C. - SABAM Belgium 2021, photography: Olivier Martin Gambier / pp. 178 – 179 © Bauhaus-Archiv Berlin for Georg Muche, photo Haus am Horn, Klassik Stiftung Weimar, photographer Thomas Müller / p. 180 © SABAM Belgium 2021 - © p. 181 © SABAM Belgium 2021 - © Bildarchiv Foto Marburg, photography: Andreas Lechtape / p. 182 © SABAM Belgium 2021 - © Kunstmuseen Krefeld - Volker Döhne – ARTOTHEK / p. 183 © Stefan Müller / pp. 184 – 185 © Museum Villa Stuck, photography: Jens Weber / pp. 186 – 187 © SABAM Belgium 2021 - © Image Select / pp. 188 – 191 © SABAM Belgium 2021 - © Stiftung Haus Schminke, photography: Ralf Ganter / p. 192 © F.L.C. - SABAM Belgium 2021 - Weissenhof UNESCO © Weissenhofmuseum / copyright Brigida Gonzalez / p. 193 © www.tautshome.com, photography: Ben Buschfeld / p. 194 © Archivio Gabriella Crespi / p. 195 © Casa Remo Brindisi / pp. 196 – 197 © Luca Sgorbini / p. 198 courtesy by Archivio Osvaldo Borsani / p. 199 © Manuel Zublena / pp. 200 – 201 © Galbi srl., photography: Andrea Grimoldi / pp. 202 – 203 © Lindman Photography / pp. 204 – 205 © Antoine van Leeuwen / p. 206 © Kim Zwarts / pp. 207 – 209 © Gea Schenk / pp. 210 – 211 © Johannes Schwartz / pp. 212 – 213 © Imre Csány - DAPH / p. 214 © SABAM Belgium 2021 - © Ossip van Duivenbode / p. 215 © SABAM Belgium 2021 - © Centraal Museum, Utrecht - Stijn Poelstra / p. 216 @ Hoge Veluwe National Park / p. 217 © Annar Bjørgli - The National Museum / pp. 218 – 219 © Polish Modern Art Foundation, photography by by Bartek Warzecha (left) and Tycjan Gniew Podskarbinski (right) / p. 221 courtesy Museum of Modern Art in Warsaw, photography: Jan Smaga / p. 222 © Paulo Guerreiro / p. 223 Serralves Villa, [south façade], 2010. Photo: Filipe Braga, © Fundação de Serralves, Porto / p. 224 © Image Select / p. 225 © SABAM Belgium 2021 - © Denis Esakov / p. 226 © Matevž Paternoster / p. 227 © Torben Eskerod / p. 229 top © Pere Vivas Ortiz - TRIANGLE POSTALS - Casa Batlló – Gaudí - Barcelona / p. 229 bottom © Catalunya La Pedrera Foundation / p. 230 © Casa Vicens Gaudí, Barcelona 2019. David Cardelus photography / pp. 231 – 233 Courtesy of Ricardo Bofill Taller de Arquitectura / p. 234 © Nomad Studio / p. 235 © OFFICE Kersten Geers David Van Severen, photography : Bas Princen / p. 236 © SABAM Belgium 2021 - © Fundacion César Manrique / p. 237 © Rudolf Steiner Archive Dornach, Switzerland - © SABAM Belgium 2021 - p. 238 © F.L.C. - SABAM Belgium 2021 - Photo E. Perroud / p. 239 © F.L.C. - SABAM Belgium 2021 / p. 240 © Image Select / p. 241 © Lakeland Arts / p. 242 © Penelope Fewster / p. 243 © Image Select / pp. 244 – 245 © National Trust for Scotland / p. 246 © John Gollings / pp. 247 – 249 © Bart Borghesi / pp. 251 – 253 © SABAM Belgium 2021 © Penelope Seidler, architect: Harry Seidler

In the same series

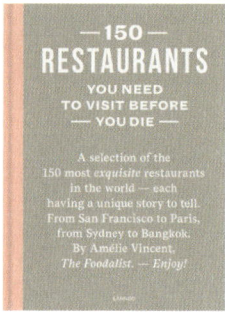

150 Restaurants
You Need to Visit
Before You Die
ISBN 9789401454421

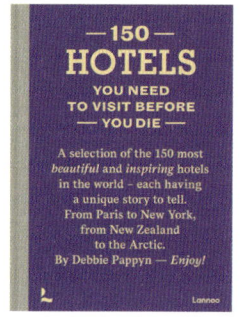

150 Hotels
You Need to Visit
Before You Die
ISBN 9789401458061

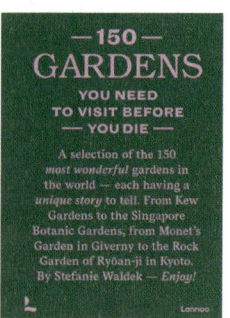

150 Gardens
You Need to Visit
Before You Die
ISBN 9789401479295

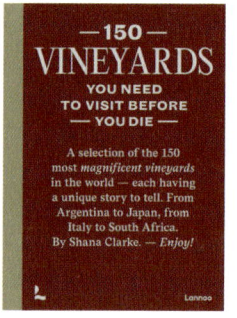

150 Vineyards
You Need to Visit
Before You Die
ISBN 9789401485463

150 Golf Courses
You Need to Visit
Before You Die
ISBN 9789401481953

150 Bars
You Need to Visit
Before You Die
ISBN 978940144912 0

Colophon

Texts
Thijs Demeulemeester
Jacinthe Gigou

Translation
Lisa Holden
Duncan Brown

Copy-editing
Breandán Kearney

Book Design
ASB

Sign up for our newsletter with news about new and forthcoming publications on art, interior design, food & travel, photography and fashion as well as exclusive offers and events. If you have any questions or comments about the material in this book, please do not hesitate to contact our editorial team: art@lannoo.com

© Lannoo Publishers, Belgium, 2021
D/2021/45/151 – NUR 648/640
ISBN: 978 94 014 6204 4
3rd print run

www.lannoo.com

All rights reserved. No part of this publication may be reproduced or transmitted in any form or by any means, electronic or mechanical, including photocopy, recording or any other information storage and retrieval system, without prior permission in writing from the publisher.

Every effort has been made to trace copyright holders. If, however, you feel that you have inadvertently been overlooked, please contact the publishers.

Note regarding all John Lautner houses: note that most, if not all, properties/structures are in private ownership hands. Please do not trespass on to the sites or disrupt the owners activities and maintenance of these historic structures. If you wish to determine if tours are or site visitation can be arranged please contact the owners via emails of posted letters, or contact the architect's representative, such as The John Lautner Foundation or others.